HACKING ELITE
COLLEGE ADMISSIONS

HACKING ELITE COLLEGE ADMISSIONS

50 SURPRISING INSIGHTS ON THE COLLEGE APPLICATION PROCESS

By Gaelle Pierre-Louis,

EdM, Former College Admissions Officer

Foreword by John Branam,
Executive Director of Get Schooled Foundation

NEW DEGREE PRESS

HACKING ELITE COLLEGE ADMISSIONS
50 Surprising Insights on the College Application Process

ISBN

978-1-64137-930-4   *Paperback*
978-1-64137-724-9   *Kindle Ebook*
978-1-64137-725-6   *Digital Ebook*

I dedicate this book to all high school students who dream of furthering their education by enrolling in college. This book is dedicated to your success, to your hard work, and to your lifelong learning experiences.

CONTENTS

There is not just one attribute that colleges are looking for from applicants. In fact, we are looking for students who have different skills and talents in order to build a brilliant and diverse class. We compare this to an orchestra. An orchestra recruits musicians with different instrumental talents in order to make a beautiful sound. An orchestra with just violin players is not enough. Similarly, a college needs students with a variety of talents, skills, and backgrounds in order to achieve its higher education mission.

—EXPLORING COLLEGE OPTIONS*

---

* Exploring College Options is a special recruitment program sponsored by the undergraduate admissions offices at five of the country's leading universities: Duke University, Georgetown University, Harvard University, the University of Pennsylvania, and Stanford University.

ABOUT THE AUTHOR

Gaelle Pierre-Louis, EdM, is a former college admissions officer and author of *Hacking College Admission: 50 Surprising Insights on the College Application & Financial Aid Process.* She holds a bachelor's degree in foreign service from Georgetown University and a master's in education from Harvard University. During her time working as an admissions officer at Georgetown University, she read and evaluated over two thousand applications for undergraduate admission and made admit, deny, defer, and waitlist recommendations to the Dean of Admissions. She also traveled extensively, speaking to large audiences of students, parents, and school counselors about the undergraduate admissions process. When she is not sharing her expertise with others, she enjoys playing piano and traveling.

FOREWORD

I love to go on early morning walks. It helps me center, and to think about my goals for the day and week ahead. Sometimes I also reflect on my journey - and the distance I've traveled from my very modest childhood in Corvallis, Oregon.

When I applied to college and matriculated in 1992, the internet did not exist. My guidance counselor was kind, but she only had time to meet with me once. During our conversation she handed me a thick book on colleges and said to return it to her in two weeks - essentially communicating that I was on my own to figure things out. Fortunately, I was determined to go to college - but the figuring-it-out part was, as is often the case for first-gens, black and brown kids and those from low-income families like mine - confusing and overwhelming. That said, I made it in and persisted through to graduation.

When I reflect on my fairly successful professional career so far, I'm extremely grateful for my family, friends and extended network. In addition, however, I attribute a significant amount of credit to my education. After earning my undergraduate degree (and coming within a day of dropping out . . . twice!),

I went on to get my law degree. And if I'm being honest, the real reason was to help ensure that as a black male, I'd have the best chance to secure the kinds of impact positions I hoped for . . . as quickly as possible. From a young age it was always clear to me that education (and degrees) would be the difference maker in my life, and given the 25 years it has been since I graduated from college, I can say with confidence that that's absolutely been the case - and a significant contributor to my ability to help provide a comfortable life for our family.

These days I'm honored to serve as the Executive Director of Get Schooled, a national nonprofit whose mission is to help young people get to college, find their first jobs, and succeed in both. We do this by providing compelling, research-based content in ways that are designed for youth consumption. Much of our content is shared via short, accessible videos, and we meet youth where they are - including on social media and via text messages where we have meaningful conversations about college and first jobs.

I believe strongly in each young person's power to achieve their full potential. This is true regardless of their zip code, their citizenship, the color of their skin or what their parents do for work. The two most significant challenges youth face in unleashing their potential are: 1) not appreciating all that they can become; and 2) not knowing where to turn for support and guidance. There are lots of different choices when it comes to college and a number of critical decisions to make, but no matter what, youth from all backgrounds *belong* in college.

I'm proud of Gaelle for her efforts in developing this useful book. Helping young people navigate through this incredibly important phase of their lives is a genuine gift. Gaelle's experiences both as a former college admissions officer and degree earner from Harvard University's Graduate School of Education enable her to offer insights and tips for all young people, and especially to those from more challenging backgrounds. There's terrific value in these pages, and it's crafted in a way that's attractive both to young people and their parents. Frankly, I wish I had this book when I was applying to college! Read it - it'll help you get into the college that's right for you, paving the way for a brighter future for you, and your family.

—John Branam
Executive Director
Get Schooled

INTRODUCTION

———

If you are a high school student right now, I know how you are feeling. To be honest, I distinctly remember what being a panicked high school senior was like—checking the online portal and mail three times a day every day for updates on my application status. I remember the feeling of taking multiple SAT and ACT practice tests every week to increase my standardized test scores. I also remember strategically stalking my teachers to figure out which ones had the time to write me the best letters of recommendation—all this while applying for every scholarship I could qualify for in order to make college affordable for my family.

If I thought the college admissions process was challenging then, it is only getting more challenging as each year goes by. As guidance counselors bear the brunt of ever-increasing workloads and admission rates decline every year at the most selective universities, many are left wondering how to stand out in this competitive admissions environment.

This is the book I wish I had read when I was applying to college because, in my honest opinion, the best advice on the process comes from those who have actually worked in admissions. Interestingly enough, my life path has taken me to the other side of the desk. After graduating from Georgetown University's School of Foreign Service, I went on to earn my master's in education policy at Harvard University and started my career off as an admissions officer at Georgetown's Office of Undergraduate Admissions, where I read thousands of applications and sat on admission committees to help choose the next class of Hoyas.

A ton of mystique and misinformation surrounds the college application process. I believe that the stress I experienced applying for college in high school stemmed from this same mystique. Generally speaking, high school students are not getting enough one-on-one time for college advising. Even students fortunate enough to have a devoted college counselor might be operating with information that was relevant ten years ago and no longer applies to modern college admissions. Nonetheless, I have realized that quality counseling could be the difference between success and failure in the admissions process. To cut through the mystery underlying the process, I have laid out this book in a myth and truth format to clarify important information and demystify what is actually going on so you can thrive in the college admissions process.

This book serves as a comprehensive guide that you can reference at every stage of the application process. It includes expert advice from countless admissions officers to help guide you with accurate information. You may be wondering if applying during the early action round or regular decision application cycle is wiser. Or you may be deciding on how many schools to apply for to maximize opportunity. You may even be wondering how to compare and negotiate scholarship packages to lessen the cost of attending college. I know this process is confusing, but this book is topic-driven and serves to give you things to consider as you make those decisions.

If you are a high school student trying to keep up with cappuccinos while balancing high school grades, this book is for you. It offers tips and advice from an experienced admissions officer in a straightforward way. You are going to find the most commonly asked questions and then the questions no one thinks to ask.

If you counsel students, I know you have a large caseload on your plate, but you are not alone, as other counselors are quoted in this book giving up-to-date advice. The process of college admissions changes rapidly, but the strategies in this book are sound and will stand the test of time. You can use this book as a tool during professional development workshops to share with other counselors and administrators at your school.

If you are a parent, college admissions have changed significantly since you went to school twenty years ago. The process is not even what it was five years ago. Regardless of whether you attended college, I know you want to help your children successfully transition to adulthood.

You are welcome to read this book from beginning to end, but I also recommend referencing the table of contents to flip to the sections you need as you see fit. If you are going to take a standardized test, skip to that section. If you are preparing to write the college essay or to ask your teacher for a recommendation letter, read over that section of the book. Ultimately, you should read it in its entirety since it contains insights you may not have thought about, but in the beginning, take a look at the topics that align with your interest.

Lastly, remember to keep an open mind when going through this process. The lessons you learn from this experience and the knowledge you acquire will serve you well in other aspects of your life. You will make some tough sacrifices in the college application process, but this book will arm you with the tools you need to succeed.

Yours truly,
Gaelle Pierre-Louis, EdM

CHAPTER 1

THE GATEKEEPERS

SECTION 1: WHO ARE THE GATEKEEPERS?

Myth: All admissions officers are old, male, and possess a high academic pedigree.

Truth: On my first day of work in the Office of Undergraduate Admissions at Georgetown University, I thought all my fellow admissions colleagues would be old, male, and highly educated with over thirty years of experience in the admissions world. Interestingly enough, that assumption was not the case. Although each one of us was highly educated, I was greeted by coworkers who were young (mid-twenties/early thirties) and diverse in gender, race, and sexual orientation. I wish more people could take a look behind the scenes and see who actually reads their application, because such insight would inform how they approach the admissions process.

The entry-level position in undergraduate admissions is the title "admissions officer," and the individuals who take on that position are typically only a few years out of college. For those who decide to make admissions their vocation, the career track starts with at least two years of learning the ropes, which consists of traveling for months out of the year to convince high school students to apply for admission and then reading and evaluating thousands of applications with the advice of the dean of admissions. After those two years, admissions officers either leave for another job or climb their way up to assistant or associate dean positions before becoming the head referred to as "dean of admissions."

Knowing admissions officers have interesting backgrounds can be liberating. This knowledge might motivate you to tell your personal story in your authentic voice. In "Secret Lives of Admissions Officers," Kathleen Kingsbury, who covers education for *The Daily Beast*, showed various portraits of admissions officers. Some highlights include William Fitzsimmons, dean of admissions and financial aid at Harvard University, who was the first generation of his family to attend college and who had to repeat ninth grade because of too many school absences. Or Wahhab Carter, associate director of enrollment at the University of Denver, who played professional basketball before joining the admissions office.[1]

On average, admissions officers at most selective universities will read over a thousand applications each per year. In the process, admissions officers are advocating for students in their territory, also known as their geographic region.

---

1   Kathleen Kingsbury, "Dirty Secrets of College Admissions," *Daily Beast*, July 14, 2017.

All admissions officers have something that makes them tick, and they use that to identify whom to advocate for in the process.

"All admissions officers have personal biases based on how we grew up," said Sara Harberson, former associate dean of admissions at the University of Pennsylvania. She added that she "was a public-school kid who had a guidance counselor who didn't know the college on my list."[2] Crystal Artist Bates, former senior assistant director of admissions at NYU, said she was always "rooting for the public school kid, who did not have a lot of resources."[3] Lori Sundberg, former application reader for Princeton University and the John Hopkins University, added that she had a soft spot for kids who grew up in poverty.[4] Other admissions officers had preferences for students who attended college preparatory boarding schools, played multiple instruments, or debated throughout high school. I knew someone who advocated for students who were homeschooled, based on her experiences as a homeschooled applicant and the uncertainties she faced when applying to college from a nontraditional background.

The process of applying to college is long and arduous. As seniors work diligently on their essays, ask teachers for recommendation letters, and gear up for a competitive application season, many people are curious:

---

2   *Vice News*, "How Broken the College Admissions Process Is (HBo)," March 13, 2019, video, 6:10.

3   Ibid.

4   Ibid.

Who are the gatekeepers with the power to admit students into their dream school?

If an admissions officer comes to your school for a college visit, be sure to take the opportunity to meet that person. They are usually the one who will give your application a first read. Take notes on what they discuss and see where your talent, background, and experiences fit into their university's goals and priorities for admission. Although having attended the school you work for is not a prerequisite, some admissions officers join the offices of their alma mater, so you can ask them questions about student life as well.

Bottom Line: While "applicants love to imagine some old men, wearing tweed, gathered in a smoke-filled room deciding who gets into college," said Kent Barnds, vice president for enrollment at Illinois's Augustana College, "in most admissions offices, that couldn't be further from the truth."[5] By understanding who these people are and what makes them tick, you will come to understand how to frame your personal story in a captivating way. Colleges care about who you are and what you are passionate about. At times, seniors in high school feel as if they should leave their true passions aside in order to impress a school. By understanding who these gatekeepers are, you will have a better overall college admissions experience. Remember that these people take note of everything—so do your best to keep every interaction as positive as possible, whether you are interacting with them via a college fair, information session, email correspondence, or phone call.

5   Kathleen Kingsbury, "Dirty Secrets of College Admissions," *Daily Beast*, July 14, 2017.

SECTION 2: WHAT IS THE ROLE OF THE GUIDANCE COUNSELOR?

Myth: The guidance counselor does not play a huge role in increasing my chance of admission.

Truth: Did you know guidance counselors are the first people admissions officers think to contact when they have any questions on your application? Did you know some admissions officers schedule counselor calls with your guidance counselor in the middle of the admissions process to ask questions about your candidacy? Did you know your guidance counselor writes you a letter of recommendation and attaches that to your application file?

Well, if you did not know that—now is your chance to start building a good rapport with your school's guidance counselor. Your guidance counselor is one of your biggest advocates in the college admissions process. Be sure to get in contact with them as early as junior year and set up at least three meetings with them before senior year, if possible. I understand some schools are under-resourced and their counselors cannot schedule more than one meeting, but you really need to attempt to meet your guidance counselor in person at least once.

Janet Lavin Rapelye, former dean of admissions at Princeton University, said guidance counselors give admissions officers "context from where the student is coming from and what has been available to them and then to talk about the student's strength."[6]

"They can be really helpful in explaining grades that are anomalies or family situations that may have adversely impacted a student," said Jacqueline Murphy, director of admission of the undergraduate program at Saint Michael's College.[7]

"At UT Austin, we use a holistic review process," said Laura Lavergne, assistant to the director at the University of Texas at Austin's Office of Admissions. "As a result, meaningful information that comes to us through any submitted items—including recommendations—[has] the potential to make a difference when we are reviewing applications."[8]

Guidance counselors also rank you based on factors such as:

- Academic growth potential
- Academic self-discipline
- Concern for others
- Energy
- Emotional maturity
- Leadership
- Reaction to setbacks
- Self-confidence

---

6   Jordan Goldman, "Do college admissions officers have relationships with HS guidance counselors?" November 17, 2014, video, 0:53.

7   Her Campus, "The Truth About Counselor Recommendation Letters," *Huffington Post*, October 27, 2014.

8   Ibid.

They also report on whether you as an applicant were found responsible for any academic infractions (violations of academic integrity and disciplinary infractions such as behavioral disconnect). According to Beth Wiser, director of admissions at the University of Vermont, students are "not at a disadvantage in applying to colleges if they are at a school where relationships cannot be built with counselors. But if you are in a position to build a good relationship with your counselor, doing so can only help you."[9]

Here are some questions to consider asking when you meet with your guidance counselors:

MEETING 1:

1. Can we review my transcript to see if I am on the right track?

2. Are there any upcoming college fairs I should know about in our area?

3. Which colleges do students from our school typically attend after graduation?

4. How can I decide on a major that aligns with my interests?

5. When is the deadline for college applications?

6. What should I include on my résumé?

9   Jordan Goldman, "Can HS Guidance counselors reach out directly to college admissions officers?" November 17, 2014, video, 2:43.

7. Are my courses rigorous enough for college?

8. Which extracurricular activities should I focus on for next year?

9. Should I refer to any college guidebooks?

10. Whom should I ask to write my letters of recommendation?

MEETING 2:
1. Can you give me advice on building my college list?

2. Should I consider taking Advanced Placement (AP) or honors courses next semester?

3. Do you recommend taking the Preliminary SAT?

4. When should I take the SAT or ACT examination?

5. How many times do you recommend taking the SAT or ACT examination?

6. Should I prepare for AP tests or SAT Subject Tests?

7. Do you offer test prep in this school?

8. How do I stack up with the rest of the students in my grade in terms of class rank?

9. When will colleges visit our school?

10. Should I consider applying early to college?

MEETING 3:

1. What are colleges looking for in my essays?

2. What are the forms I need to fill out to qualify for financial aid?

3. Do I qualify for application fee waivers?

4. Are there any special scholarships, awards, or state aid I should be aware of?

5. Will I be required to complete a college interview?

6. How many colleges can I apply to?

7. Will I still be successful in the college application process if I have been suspended from school?

8. Am I at a disadvantage if I do not physically visit colleges?

9. Should I use the Common App or Coalition App to submit my application?

10. Do you feel as if you know enough about me to write a good letter of recommendation?

Bottom Line: When I worked in admissions, guidance counselors were the first people we called if an applicant had a discrepancy in their application or if we needed more clarification about something on the application. Having a positive rapport with your guidance counselor is incredibly important. They help students develop a plan to succeed in college admissions and the financial aid process. They are your key advocates when you apply to colleges, and college admissions officers trust them to provide accurate information about your qualifications for admission. Talking to your college counselor about your goals and passions allows them to help you figure out which college will be a great fit and how to craft your college application in a way that will help you rise to the top. Get in touch with them as soon as possible, since the process of applying requires many tasks, including drafting and revising essays, arranging campus tours, and completing the Free Application for Federal Student Aid (FAFSA) and College Scholarship Service (CSS) Profile should you need to apply for financial aid. If your counselor cannot provide you a letter, ask a principal or senior administrator at your school.

SECTION 3: WHOM SHOULD I ASK TO WRITE MY COLLEGE RECOMMENDATION LETTERS?

Myth: Recommendation letters from influential people will increase my chances of admission.

Truth: During my time working in admissions, one of the most popular questions students would ask us is whether they could submit additional recommendation letters. Typically, they would use this opportunity to send a letter from a local congressperson or another influential person who vaguely knows the applicant in an effort to gain a huge edge over other applicants in the high-stakes competition for admission. Generally speaking, most of the letters from these influential figures were very generic, and we did not consider those letters an asset unless the influential figure offered a perspective that was genuinely authentic about the applicant. In the majority of applications I read, the insights provided by these letters were pretty surface level and superficial.

"We regularly receive letters from former presidents, celebrities, trustee relatives, and Olympic athletes," said Rebecca Sabky, former admissions director at Dartmouth College. "But they generally fail to provide us with another angle on who the student is, or could be, as a member of our community," she added.[10]

If someone has only met a congressperson or politician once or twice at a fundraiser, what type of insight could that person possibly provide that would not be evident in other parts of the admissions portfolio, such as materials submitted by the guidance counselor or teacher recommendations? In some cases, I noticed that the politician would typically write that they have known the family for many years and use that as the basis for writing the recommendation. Admissions offices are not admitting the family, but rather a student, based on their individual achievements.

The best letters of recommendation come from teachers. Meg Lysy, former associate director of undergraduate admissions at Georgetown University, said that "teachers that can give anecdotes about a student in the classroom can be helpful because we are trying to imagine the student in our classroom and we are wondering if this student is always speaking up

---

10   Jim Paterson, "Toward a Better Letter," NACAC, accessed June 4, 2020.

and always raising their hand."[11] She added that admissions officers are wondering, *Is this the student that the teacher would ask to watch the class if they had to leave the room for a minute, or the student who is fairly quiet and only speaks once in a while, but when the student speaks it turns the conversation around on its head?*

If you do choose to send a letter from someone who has not taught you in the classroom, try to choose someone who knows you well. Sabky, former head of admissions at Dartmouth, once described how a letter from a school janitor convinced the admissions committee to admit the applicant. The janitor wrote about the student's kindness and thoughtfulness, stating that the applicant was "the only person in the school who knew the names of every member of the janitorial staff."[12] In "over fifteen years and thirty thousand applications in my admissions career, I had never seen a recommendation from a school custodian," Sabky said. "It gave us a window onto a student's life in the moments when nothing 'counted.' That student was admitted by unanimous vote of the admissions committee." [13]

Bottom Line: Recommendation letters tie many aspects of your application together. They tell a story about the applicant. They can truly make the difference in terms of admissions and scholarship opportunities. Be sure to remember that the most important thing you can do is have genuinely authentic

---

11 College Admissions, "Elements of a strong recommendation letter," August 17, 2014, video, 2:33.

12 Jim Paterson, "Toward a Better Letter," NACAC, accessed June 4, 2020.

13 Ibid.

recommendation letters from people who know you and can speak well on your behalf. If you happen to genuinely know an influential figure and want them to vouch for you, feel free to have them write you a letter of recommendation. The young actress Yara Shahidi was lucky enough to get former first lady Michelle Obama to write her a letter of recommendation after visiting and speaking on panels at the White House numerous times. However, if you do not have recommendation letters from famous people, your application can still stand out, since the ones from an academic teacher and your guidance counselor truly do suffice. Remember that admissions officers not only read every line the recommender writes, but they are also able to read between the lines. So, be sure to choose recommenders who know you best and can write extensively about their personal knowledge of you and your work inside and outside of the classroom.

SECTION 4: IS RECEIVING HELP FROM COLLEGE ADMISSIONS CONSULTANTS OKAY?

Myth: A college advising consultant can guarantee me admission to a top-tier school if I pay them a certain amount of money.

Truth: Absolutely not! Picture this scenario: You are reading a file, and the student athlete applicant seems stellar—great grades, near perfect test scores, fantastic letters of recommendation, and ample athletic talent. Then you call their high school guidance counselor with a few questions about the application, only to realize everything written on the application contains information that is not true. What would you do?

The world of college admissions consulting is now one of the fastest-growing industries in education, with millions of dollars in revenue every year. In this largely unregulated industry, you need to know which consultants are legitimate. Remember that a college consultant can never guarantee admission to a university, and if they tell you they can, they are scamming you, which could lead to long-term consequences.

On Tuesday, March 12, 2019, federal prosecutors from the Department of Justice brought charges against more than fifty people in a college bribery scandal, wherein wealthy parents allegedly paid about $25 million to a for-profit college counseling organization to help their children gain admittance to prestigious colleges.[14] If a college consultant tries to help you cheat on standardized tests, bribes athletic coaches and college admissions officers at the university on your behalf, or tells you they have a guarantee if you pay a certain amount of money, run fast. The world of college admissions is quite small, and the backlash you will receive from working with such an individual is not worth the cost, as we have seen with this recent scandal.

"If a student is unqualified, there's no secret sauce to get into an Ivy League," said Mark Sklarow, CEO of the Independent Educational Consultants Association (IECA), a professional organization that represents two thousand education consultants. "Our job is to understand the student [and] find what school they're the right fit for. Obviously,

---

14   Justice Department, "Affidavit In Support of Criminal Complaint," accessed June 4, 2020.

college applications create tremendous anxiety for parents and students."[15]

Not all college consultants are unethical. Some truly do proper, ethical work to help high school students navigate the increasingly complex college admissions world. Here are five things to look out for when choosing an admissions consultant to work with on your application:

1. Seek references from those they have coached in the past. Ask their previous students questions about their approach to college admissions.

2. Do they belong to a national college counseling group and attend national conferences for ethical college admissions?

3. Do they have a good online presence or are they hiding their consulting services behind closed doors?

4. Do they charge exorbitant fees for their service that cost more than the tuition for attending college at your dream school?

5. Have they worked inside an admissions office at a reputable school?

Bottom Line: You can get help on your college application, but make sure it is done the legal way. No exact formula exists

---

15 Jonathan Ng, "Admissions consultants warn of red flags," *Boston Herald*, March 12, 2019.

to gain acceptance into prestigious universities. Do not let people convince you of quick schemes, since they are probably not a legitimate service. A statement from the president of Stanford University reads that "applicants to Stanford sign a statement verifying that the information they are providing is accurate" and "[if] it is found to be inaccurate, they can be dis-enrolled from the university or have their admission cancelled, as has regretfully happened in the past."[16] Thus, when you apply to a university, you are opting to adhere to an honor code. If you are found guilty of dishonoring the code, consequences include facing serious disciplinary actions. Ultimately, the role of a college advising consultant should be to guide a student to find the college that best fits based on that student's skills and interests and to help them take ownership of an increasingly complex college application process.

SECTION 5: HOW CAN I EFFECTIVELY COMMUNICATE WITH COACHES AS A STUDENT ATHLETE APPLICANT?

Myth: College coaches can contact me any time they want, and I can do the same as well.

Truth: The rules surrounding when and how coaches can contact you are stringent. A coach can only send you brochures/ literature and contact you during a certain period of time. According to Next College Student Athlete (NCSA), neither student athletes nor coaches can initiate phone conversations until June 15 during the student athlete's sophomore year or

---

16 *Stanford News*, "Stanford information on college admissions case," March 14, 2019.

September 1 of junior year, depending on the sport and the division level. [17]

Half of high school students—about eight million—play a high school sport. However, only roughly 480,000 students compete as NCAA athletes.[18] Although NCAA athletes earn college degrees at higher rates, being recruited to a Division I sport at a selective university is difficult, so you must plan ahead.

Given that the recruitment of athletes has become more competitive over the years, coaches now play a more important role in the admissions process than ever before. Whereas before, college students used to be able to get into college academically and "walk on" to teams, now that system is few and far between. Being recruited on a team as an athlete certainly gives you a tip in the admissions process, but you still have to be competitive to get the final letter. Unlike with traditional applicants, athletic recruiting usually starts earlier in your high school career.

Typically, the office of admissions works with the coach to make sure the athlete whom the coach is recruiting is also excelling academically. To that end, coaches and the sport's admissions representative maintain communication throughout the process to ensure the athlete being recruited will succeed in college both inside and outside of the classroom.

---

17   Next College Student Athlete, "NCAA Recruiting Rules: When Can College Coaches Contact High School Athletes," accessed June 4, 2020.

18   NCAA, "Estimated probability of competing in college athletics," accessed June 4, 2020.

Claudine Gay, who overseas Harvard athletics, released a statement that explained Harvard's process for recruiting athletes. She stated that first, "the applications of all recruited student athletes are reviewed by the full admissions committee and decisions are made through a vote of the entire committee. The committee has approximately 40 members."[19] She then added that "all recruited student athletes must be interviewed by an admissions officer or alumni interviewer."

Because recruitment has become a more competitive process, applicants can be overlooked by coaches despite their skills. As a result, you must know the best ways to communicate with coaches in an appropriate and timely fashion.

Before that date, athletes can start light communication by emailing coaches of programs they are interested in as early as possible. NCSA suggests you send them your athletic résumé, which includes:

- Your highlight video
- Any sport-specific stats
- Your academic information
- Why you are interested in their program

Notre Dame men's lacrosse coach Kevin Corrigan said you should email coaches frequently when you are finally allowed to. He stated, "You are not trying to be an annoyance, but you do want to be an irritant who wants coaches to see you. We all remember who those guys are. They want to be aware of

---

19 Harvard Faculty of Arts and Sciences, "A message about Harvard Athletics," Harvard University, April 4, 2019.

you before junior year, in which you cannot talk to coaches. We want to know where you are academically to see if you are a good fit."[20]

By doing so, you will be on the radar of interested coaches when the NCAA recruiting rules allow the coaches to contact you.

By your junior year, you can:

1. Meet with the coach in person.

2. Meet with admissions representatives.

3. Do research on the web.

4. Fill out and return the questionnaire for your sport.

5. Contact the coach and ask any questions you might have.

6. Schedule an official visit.

Having an online profile is critical for athletes to get evaluated early. Given the recent athletic admissions scandal, now more than ever you need an online footprint. Your online profile is also your online résumé in many ways. Ask your athletic coach to help you draft an athletic résumé. In many situations, the admissions officer makes the admission decision based on the recommendation of the coach. So take the college

---

20 Notre Dame Lacrosse, "The Recruiting Series Episode 8: Communication from Recruits to Coaches," April 8, 2020, video, 2:41.

application part seriously. You must still meet the academic requirements necessary for the top recruits.

Bottom Line: Although you might be tempted to reach out to college coaches as early as possible in your high school career, you should read the rules and regulations from the NCAA about doing so before actually reaching out. First impressions last, and you want to make sure you are doing the right thing at the right time. Remember that a "verbal commitment" by a coach is NOT enough to assume you have been offered admission. The offer from an admissions officer is the only one that is valid, especially at the Division I level. As the competition stiffens for student athlete spots on campus, you should ideally connect with your high school coach and guidance counselor first instead of simply making decisions on your own about the process.

Be sure to visit the NCAA recruiting rules on its website, as it carefully details when contact can be initiated and in what capacity you can initiate those interactions. In light of the college admissions scandal, in which applicants were gaining fraudulent admissions spots as student athletes even when they could not play the sport, colleges are now asking for athletic résumés, highlight videos, and more letters of recommendation for your sport before making admissions decisions.

CHAPTER 2

PREPARE FOR SUCCESS

—

SECTION 6: WHAT IS THE BEST WAY TO DEMONSTRATE INTEREST IN MY DREAM SCHOOL?

Myth: I do not need to show interest in my dream school to get acceptance.

Truth: Many students are told they must visit their first-choice university, sign up for all of their mailing lists, and call the admissions office every week to get noticed by admissions officers at their dream school. The truth is that not all universities track demonstrated interest. According to Inside Higher Ed, the term "demonstrated interest" refers to ways in which applicants show they are serious about enrolling at a given college.[21]

Some universities track all your interactions with them and include that in their decision-making. Katie Erikson,

---

21   Scott Jaschik, "Another Edge for the Wealthy," *Inside Higher Ed*, July 27, 2017.

an assistant director of admissions at American University, said now more than ever, students are "connecting with colleges and universities digitally, and colleges want to hear from students who have interacted with them during the admissions process."[22] She added that these interactions can be as "simple as emailing their admissions representative, visiting the campus, and seeing the information session and a guided walking tour, or do[ing] an admissions interview."[23]

In addition, Boston University tracks interest: "Each time a student sees us at an event, we note that they've taken an extra step to learn more about us," said Emily Lake, associate director of admissions at Boston University. "Applying early decision is a great option for students who know that BU is their first choice because it is the ultimate way to demonstrate interest in BU." [24]

Other schools will tell you that demonstrating interest in their college does not factor into their evaluation of your application. For example, Georgetown University, Stanford University, and Harvard University explicitly tell applicants that demonstrating interest by visiting campus, liking their social media, etc., does not factor into their holistic review of an applicant's file.

---

22 American University Admissions, "What AU Looks For: Demonstrated Interest," September 23, 2019, video, 2:23.

23 Ibid.

24 Boston University, "Alumni Admissions Volunteers—Volunteer Handbook," 2019-2020.

Whether or not the universities on your college list count demonstrated interest, here are some actions you can take to stand out in the admissions process and seem on top of it:

1. Attend high school visits at your school's guidance counselor office.

Your high school's college guidance office will typically have flyers that notify students on when admissions officers from various universities will visit your school. Take advantage of that opportunity to meet with admissions officers.

2. Go to a college fair.

College fairs are typically held in the fall and spring for prospective students and they offer these students an opportunity to learn more about a university and ask questions of admissions representatives.

3. Visit schools and attend the information session and tour.

If you have the time and resources, visiting campus is helpful. Admissions officers typically give information sessions that last about an hour, immediately followed by a campus tour with current undergraduate students.

4. Watch the webinars or Facebook Live events for the colleges you are interested in attending.

Typically, online webinars through social media sites are offered as an alternative to the information session and tour model, which are a great option for students who cannot visit in person.

5. Participate in an alumni interview, even if it is "optional."

The last remaining face-to-face opportunity to get your voice heard in college admissions is the alumni interview. Typically, these alumni live in your local area and volunteer their time to meet with prospective students and write a one-page report on your personal qualities. If this option is available to you, take it!

6. Reach out to an admissions officer via email.

While students should not email their regional admissions office on a weekly basis, certain times may be appropriate to message an admissions representative for maximum impact. Typically, following up with a note after a college fair, information session, or a tour never hurts. You can also write your regional admissions officer to provide any updates or achievements you receive throughout the year. Ask your guidance teacher for help writing that update letter!

7. Open emails from the school.

Colleges can typically see if you receive their emails. They have software that not only lets them see whether you open their email, but also how many times you have opened it.

8. Write about your interest in the essay portion.

Most universities have a supplementary essay they require which basically ask: Why X college? Why Columbia? Why Georgetown? Why Harvard?

9. Apply early decision to your dream school.

Early decision is the process by which you apply to your dream school by November 1 and hear back by mid-December whether you have been accepted. If accepted, you are legally bound to attend that school, so make sure it is your first choice.

10. Send updates throughout the year.

If you won an award, academic honor, or competition, be sure to write your colleges and let them know. They appreciate hearing about your new achievements throughout the year.

Bottom Line: Depending on the schools you plan to apply to, demonstrating interest by opening emails, visiting campus, and applying early decision may show admissions officers that you are interested and give you an edge in the admissions process. Be sure to ask colleges if they track demonstrated interest and follow the guidelines listed above on how to stand out in the admissions process.

SECTION 7: WHICH QUESTIONS SHOULD I ASK DURING A COLLEGE TOUR OR INFORMATION SESSION?

> **Myth:** If I do not have any questions, I should stay quiet instead of asking stupid questions.

Truth: In the world of admissions, stupid questions simply do not exist. The college application process is increasingly more complex every single year, and there is always new information you need clarified in order to know how to proceed. You are never bothering an admissions officer by asking questions. In fact, asking questions is highly encouraged during your information sessions and college tours.

So, you may be asking, *What are college tours and information sessions?*

Campus tours are usually held by the current students at that school. They provide an opportunity to walk around campus for about an hour, introduce you to the buildings and classrooms, and offer unique insight on what being a student is like at that university. A tour is a great opportunity to ask questions about the day-to-day life in the university.

Information sessions are presentations given by the admissions officer of the university. They typically last forty-five minutes to an hour prior to the campus tour. In the information session, the admissions officer typically gives a brief overview of the history of the school, the course offerings available to undergraduate students, and then the admissions requirements necessary to enter the school. After the admissions officer presents, they usually provide about fifteen to twenty minutes for questions before the tour starts.

If you're in the process of planning your information session and tour, be sure to:

1. Call the admissions office or look on the website for the link to schedule a visit up to four weeks in advance. Tens of thousands of students visit universities every single day, so you must schedule in advance, as these visits fill up really quickly.

2. Be sure to research the university on its website. Doing some research about the school before arriving helps you get context for the information you will be hearing.

3. Notify the admissions office if your plan changes. Canceling the session is okay as long as you let them know at least twenty-four to forty-eight hours in advance—which also gives you a better chance of rescheduling. Some colleges track demonstrated interest of prospective applicants in their decision-making, so you want to make a great first impression.

Once you're at the information session:

1. Silence your phone and do not take any photographs or videos when you are listening to the information session. Encourage your parents and siblings to follow those rules as well. Someone's phone ringing during the session is really distracting and can interrupt the admissions officer's presentation.

2. When you are asking questions in the group session, ask general questions and save the personal question for one-on-one sessions.

3. Be sure to not have any private conversation with your parents or siblings while listening to the information session. These conversations disrupt the other parents and the flow of the presentation.

4. Remember to ask for the admissions officer's card after the information session and email them with questions you may have or to reiterate your interest in the school.

While you're still on your campus tour:

1. Remember to figure out who your regional admissions officer is and ask when they will be traveling to your local area.

2. Be respectful to the current student who guides you through the campus tour.

3. Take the time to walk on campus after the tour and ask students on campus what they think.

Here are some questions you may ask as you attend these tours and information sessions:

Campus Tour (with student)

1. Why did you choose to attend this school?

2. What was your transition like from high school to college?

3. What is your experience like in the dining hall?

4. Who is your favorite professor and why?

5. How easy was it for you to make friends here?

6. How many clubs and extracurricular activities have you joined during your time here?

7. What is one thing you wish you could have changed about your freshman year here?

8. Is the campus safe, especially at night?

9. Does your campus recognize sororities or fraternities?

10. Do you get to choose your roommates and dorm situation?

Information Session (with admissions officer)

1. Which majors are the most popular on your campus?

2. How can undergraduate students get involved in research opportunities?

3. Do you know what the process is like for study abroad?

4. Is your school score choice for standardized testing?

5. How does geographic diversity play a role in your admissions process?

6. Who are the most popular employers for your graduates?

7. Do you require the alumni interview?

8. Do you track demonstrated interest?

9. What are your early action and early decision policies?

10. Are you need-blind in your admissions process?

Bottom Line: Familiarizing yourself with what you need to know will be helpful for you as you move on in the process.

If you can afford to do so, visit college campuses to meet with current students and admissions officers. If you are going with a large group, you need to sign up early. Nat Smitobol—who previously worked in admissions at Skidmore College, New York University, and NYU Abu Dhabi—suggests calling to schedule your visit up to three weeks in advance.[25] Tours are a great starting point as you build your college list.

SECTION 8: HOW IMPORTANT IS SOCIAL MEDIA PRESENCE IN THE COLLEGE PROCESS?

> **Myth:** Admissions officers do not check my online footprint (social media) at any point during the admissions process.

Truth: You might be wondering, *What is an online footprint?* Simply put, it is all the information someone can find about you when they search your name online. During my time as an admissions officer at Georgetown, I rarely checked a student's social media in order to make a decision. However, I vividly remember being forced to check a student's online profile because of a bad alumni interview report. This student earned top grades at a prestigious boarding school, but the interviewer wrote that the student had poor character and needed to clean up his online profile before applying to colleges because it was horrendous. I ended up taking a look and realized this student had some information online that was quite problematic. After the admissions committee took

---

25   Nat Smitobol, "Tips for College Visit Information Sessions," Ivywise, March 24, 2015.

a look at the situation, he did not get admitted. Although the negative report was not the only reason why he was denied admission, it did not help his case, especially in a competitive pool in which other candidates had stellar grades without the bad interview reports.

"As a residential campus, when we're reviewing candidates, we're just not admitting students for the classroom; we're admitting students to be a part of this community," said Marilyn Hesser, executive director of admissions at the University of Richmond in Virginia. "The University of Richmond doesn't look at an applicant's social media accounts," Hesser said, "unless the student sends links highlighting profiles." [26]

The best action students can take to improve their online footprint and put their best foot forward is:

1. **Do not change your name on Facebook, Instagram, or Twitter.** If someone tries to look you up, they should find your real account, because there are many imposters out there who might pretend to be you and ruin your image. Bradley S. Shear, a lawyer specializing in social media law, stated that colleges might "erroneously identify the account of a person with the same name as a prospective student— or even mistake an impostor account—as belonging to the applicant, potentially leading to unfair treatment."[27]

---

26 Josh Moody, "Why Colleges Look at Students' Social Media," *U.S. News & World Report*, August 22, 2019.

27 Natasha Singer, "They Loved Your G.P.A. Then They Saw Your Tweets," *The New York Times*, November 9, 2013.

2. **Delete alcohol-related posts on social media.** This advice may go beyond alcohol to other substances, especially given that we live in a time where some substances are legal in some places and illegal in others—which is something for applicants to consider if they are applying out of state.

3. **Create socially acceptable email addresses to use during the process.** Please use a professional-sounding email that you actively check while interacting with admissions officers.

4. **Do not send a friend request on social media to an admissions officer, and that includes LinkedIn.** Doing so is simply not appropriate. An incident occurred at Pitzer College in which an admissions officer befriended an applicant on Facebook and noticed an offensive post about his teachers. That admissions officer brought the evidence to the admissions committee and they thought, "This is not the kind of person we want in our community," Angel B. Perez, Pitzer's dean of admissions and financial aid, told me. "With about 4,200 applications annually for a first-year class of 250 students, the school can afford to be selective."[28]

Bottom Line: Social media can be both a blessing and a curse in the college admissions process. Admissions officers may check your online presence via social media, so keep yours professional, especially when you are applying to colleges.

---

28   Ibid.

Associate VP for Enrollment Management at Southern Methodist University Wes Waggoner said, "There have been cases where what you see on someone's social media page made them the wrong fit for the university."[29] You do not have to delete your social media accounts or change your name on social media. Essentially, if someone looks you up, they should be able to find you and see that you are a normal teenager. Most likely, the admissions officer will not have a reason to look you up, but if they do, make sure your online presence matches the personality and information you show in your application. This consideration is great preparation not only for the college admissions, but also for the job and internship process.

SECTION 9: WHAT IS THE PROTOCOL AROUND SENDING GIFTS IN THE COLLEGE PROCESS?

> **Myth:** Giving the admissions office a gift will show them how interested I am in attending and increase my chances of getting admitted.

Truth: In addition to submitting their college applications, many applicants also feel the need to submit extravagant gifts to the dean of admissions or regional admissions officer at their dream school. Honestly, that move is a huge faux pas. In the process of applying to colleges, many prospective students are seeking ways to stand out in the admissions process. But you have to make sure you are standing out in the right ways.

---

29 *CBS News*, "Social media and college admissions," video, 1:18. December 18, 2014.

Do not waste your time sending in gifts, because they might actually affect you negatively. Some ask whether sending gifts work to increase your chances of admissions, and the answer is no, according to Debra Shaver, director of admissions at Smith College. "While these gifts do entertain the staff, they do nothing to help you get accepted!"[30]

"In fact, most of them get tossed right in the trash," added Shaver. "If anything, a gift may HURT your chances—if you cross the line of good taste."[31]

All your interactions with the university are saved to your application file, so putting your best foot forward is in your best interest. Instead of sending gifts, a thank-you note by email or by mail is much more appropriate. Keeping mail from prospective students in the applicant pool is typically against office policy. A gift usually does not change the admissions committee's opinion about your application, and it might slightly annoy your regional admissions officer. If you are an applicant on the cusp, sending a gift actually might make it harder for the admissions committee to accept you, because they do not want to seem biased toward you against the other candidates who did not submit cookies, for example. Admissions officers do their best to make the process fair for everyone, and most of the time, if you simply submit your application by the deadline, that is enough to get full consideration for your candidacy.

---

30 Tesh, "Giving Gifts to the Admissions Department Could Actually Hurt Your Chances of Getting into College," *Intelligence for Your Life*, accessed June 4, 2020.

31 Ibid.

Here is a sample thank you letter:

Dear [Admission's Officer Name],

I hope this note finds you well. I wanted to
use this opportunity to thank you for taking
the time to give me such a great information
session today and for introducing me to
the offerings and my options here at [Name
of University].

It was a pleasure to meet you and hear your
response to the questions I asked on my tour.
This university is my first-choice school and I
will be applying here in the fall. I look forward
to submitting my application to your university
and hearing from you next spring.

All my best,

[Your Name]

Bottom line: Giving gifts is typically seen as bribery; giving
gifts to an admissions officer is not appropriate. Trust me—
do not send food, gifts, tickets, or money, especially when a
simple thank-you note by mail or email would suffice. "Is it
necessary to write a thank-you note?" said Janet L. Rapelye,

dean of admissions at Princeton. "No. But I'm still in favor of them. Expressing gratitude is a lovely quality."[32] Be sure to ask for advice from a counselor and take heed of the guidance in this book about the best ways to stand out. Receiving a personalized thank-you note makes a difference. All communication between you and the admissions office goes directly into your application file. If the college does not explicitly ask you to send something extra with your application, do not do so, because it creates more work for the admissions staff and distracts them from looking at the important parts of your application. You should send guidance counselors and teachers who have written you a letter of recommendation a thank-you note as well.

SECTION 10: HOW SHOULD I PREPARE FOR COLLEGE INTERVIEWS?

> **Myth:** College interviews do not matter as much as they used to, especially if they are optional.

Truth: In this day and age, few colleges require the interview portion of the application. But, if you do have the opportunity to interview during your application process, I would tell you to take advantage of it for a variety of reasons.

If you do your research and see that most of the applicants who apply take part in an alumni interview, then you should

---

32   Karen W Arenson, "Thank-You Note Enters College Admission Game," *The New York Times*, October 9, 2007.

also sit for an interview to show that you took all the necessary steps to "complete" your application. If you do not sit for an interview, the school may read that as you are not interested in attending the school, especially when demonstrated interest is being taken into account.

"We've had colleges that will say to us, 'Your students are within two hours of us. So, unless you know they're from a low-income background and don't have the opportunity to come to us, we're going to expect them to come,'" said Sean Logan, dean of college counseling at Phillips Academy and former admissions officer at Harvard, Stanford, and Occidental College.[33]

If you cannot make an in-person interview, you have other options. Let the institution know your situation, and they might be able to set up an alternative solution, such as a Skype or even phone interview.

"What you want to do to prepare yourself is not think of it as a formal job interview, but an opportunity for you to learn more about the institution and to discuss your interest in that institution," expressed the former assistant dean for diversity and outreach at Stanford University.[34]

---

33 College Admission, "Succeeding at the college admissions interview," August 17, 2014, video, 6:22.

34 Ibid.

Here are some other ways to prepare for the interview.

1. Do your homework on the school.

Be prepared to talk about the college and how your interest fits the program offerings at the university and how you can contribute to the campus community. Make sure to highlight some professors you admire and some of the courses you might be interested in taking based on the course catalog.

2. Learn how to talk about your résumé.

Bring up what you like to do inside and outside of school. Tell the interviewer something that might not come up on the essay or résumé sheet. The best way to prepare for this is by answering this question: "How would your best friend describe you?" Admissions interviewers are advised to "encourage students to share parts of themselves they were not able to—or did not feel comfortable enough to—discuss on their application," says Dr. Shirag Shemmassian, former Cornell admissions interviewer.[35] This interview is not a license to overshare. However, you could bring up a personal difficulty that led to low grades during sophomore year or a hobby that occupies a significant amount of time. The interviewer will then report that information to the school for consideration.

---

35 Shirag Shemmassian, "6 steps to ace a college interview, according to an expert who worked in Ivy League admissions," *Business Insider*, November 15, 2018.

3. Talk about your personal family life.

If appropriate, discuss information about your family life. Sometimes, students qualify for scholarships geared toward first-generation students, for example, based on what they say in their interview. You should definitely note privacy concerns. Always remember that disclosing family details is never absolutely necessary. But, if certain information can be helpful in understanding the full picture of your application, share what you need to.

4. Prepare questions for your interviewer.

Come prepared with questions to ask that interviewer, and do not ask them generic questions you can get out of the guidebook. For example, do not ask the interviewer about the majors available, but instead inquire which major they chose and how they leveraged their knowledge in that major to get their first job.

Bottom Line: Although fewer colleges require the interview portion today, it is still an important opportunity to add value to your application, especially when you are applying to highly selective colleges. Nowadays, most of these interviews are conducted by the university's alumni, who volunteer their time and energy to provide feedback to admissions offices. Even if the alumni interview portion is optional, you should still sit for one if you can. Although some try to dismiss the college interview as not being as important as it used to be, keep in mind that in these competitive application pools, you have to do more rather than less to stand out.

CHAPTER 3

APPLY, APPLY, APPLY

SECTION 11: WHICH IS THE BETTER OPTION: COMMON APPLICATION VS. COALITION APPLICATION?

> **Myth:** The application platform I should use depends on the number of schools I am applying to.

Truth: You have two application platforms you may use to complete your college application—the Common and Coalition applications. You should use the application platform based on whether the schools on your college list accept them. To begin thinking about this question, make a spreadsheet of all the schools you plan to apply to. Visit the school's website and look for their admissions policies and procedures. You need to check which schools take which application platforms. Beware that some schools only take their own college-specific application and do not use application platforms, such as Georgetown University and MIT. For those schools, you will have to apply directly on that college's website.

Depending on the schools on your list, you may have to use more than one platform simultaneously. The **Common Application** is a platform from which a student may apply to any of more than eight hundred colleges and universities around the world.[36] Before the Common App, students had to request an application from each school on their list and then mail them back individually. With the Common App, you can fill out one main application and then personalize the supplementary materials for each school on your college list. You will not have to mail anything to your colleges, since the Common App will take care of sending everything electronically.

The **Coalition Application** is a platform featuring 150 distinguished colleges and universities that are committed to making college a reality for all high school students through online planning tools that help students learn about, prepare for, and apply to college.[37] The Coalition App does not replace the Common App. In fact, sometimes you will need to apply through both application platforms, depending on the schools on your list. The Coalition App can also serve as a backup to send your application. If you are using the Common App and it breaks down or something does not go through, you can potentially send materials through the Coalition Application.

Both platforms are free to use and employ similar prompts, so choose the one that best suits your needs for the college application process. Heidi Meyer, executive director of admissions

---

36   Common App, 2020.

37   The Coalition for College, 2020, *Coalition for College Access.*

at the University of Minnesota, Twin Cities, stated, "We want students to use whatever application best fits their life and where they are planning on attending or applying for school."[38]

The time needed to fill out a college application will vary based on the requirements for each school. However, students "need to give themselves at least six weeks to get everything they need for college applications," said Christine Chu, a former admissions officer at Yale University. "That's two weeks to fill out any background information and at least a month for other required documents."[39] Everything you do on these platforms will automatically save and reopen when you log onto the app until you are ready to submit. Once you submit the documents, you cannot edit through the app, but you will be able to email changes to the schools directly.

Bottom Line: As a result of advancing technologies, the process is becoming easier for students to apply for college. As a result, schools are receiving more applications. The Common App and the Coalition App have minor differences in requirements, but you will have no significant advantage in using one application over the other. Based on the admission requirements for the schools on your college list, feel free to choose the college application platform that is right for you. For both platforms, give yourself between four to six weeks to complete the application process. Save plenty of time to receive recommendation letters, as your application is typically not complete and submitted until everything is

38   Briana Bovington and Josh Moody, "The Common App: Everything You Need to Know," *U.S. News & World Report*, August 1, 2019.

39   Ibid.

available. The more time you leave before the deadline, the easier a time you will have completing your application and sending everything on time. If you have any questions, you can reach out to the customer service department of these platforms for advice.

SECTION 12: SHOULD I SUBMIT SUPPLEMENTARY MATERIALS TO COLLEGES?

Myth: I should not bother submitting "optional" supplementary materials.

Truth: While admissions officers place a greater weight on required materials like college essays and standardized test scores, supplementary materials are welcomed if they add a new perspective that is not demonstrated in other parts of the application. In fact, even if a school says something is optional, if you want to stand out, you should submit it.

Janet L. Rapelye, former dean of admissions at Princeton University, once said that "it is important to read the fine print on an application to see whether or not the college accepts extra pieces of information."[40] She went on to add, "A few years ago, Princeton's music director/conductor went to me and said, 'We need more brass musicians for the orchestra, and if we do not admit brass musicians, the orchestra will be in trouble.'"[41] So, Princeton's admissions staff started

---

40   Jordan Goldman, "Do College admissions officers pay attention to extra materials students send?" November 17, 2014, video, 2:14.

41   Ibid.

looking for students who could play brass instruments. They sifted through music supplements that applicants sent them and found terrific talent as rated by these CDs and videos of students playing brass instruments. As long as they did well enough academically, they were able to get admitted to Princeton simply because their talents became an institutional priority. "It actually changed the repertoire of what the orchestra could do the next year," Rapelye said. "But you are not necessarily going to know what talents they are looking for in a given year. As anything in this process, there are no guarantees, but if you have talents, let us know."[42]

Depending on the school, supplemental materials may include:

- Audio recordings
- Art samples/portfolios
- Musical scores
- Writing samples
- Short films
- Dance videos
- Academic/scientific research papers
- Research abstracts
- Extra letters of recommendation
- Updates regarding:
  - Awards received
  - Championships won
  - Participation in certain events
- Expanded high school résumé
- Newspaper articles that feature you

---

42   Ibid.

If you have a well-developed talent that is not showcased in other parts of the application, please consider submitting a supplementary material as listed above.

Before you submit college supplements, here are some things to consider:

1. Check the college's rules and regulations around supplementary materials.

2. Consider who will review it, whether a faculty member or admissions officer, and write down their contact information.

3. Follow the instructions on how to submit it. Be sure to review the guidelines on the website.

4. Speak with your guidance counselor before submitting. They will help you strategize and prepare materials.

Bottom Line: You never know what colleges are looking for in any given year, so if you have special skills and talents, feel free to share them with the admissions committee. Do not go overboard and submit long research papers or videos so large they become boring to watch, or even worse, cause a virus to attack their computer. Instead, you can submit a single-page research abstract or summaries of your awards and recognitions as supplements. Supplementary materials are supposed to help highlight talents, awards, and recognitions that admissions officers would not have seen in other aspects of your application. Every school has their policy, so be sure to read them before submitting extra materials.

If a school does not accept supplementary materials, do not send anything. Keep in mind the deadline when submitting materials to your colleges.

SECTION 13: SHOULD I TAKE THE SAT OR THE ACT EXAMINATION?

> **Myth:** Highly selective universities prefer the SAT examination over the ACT examination.

Truth: Most students begin standardized test preparation and planning during their junior year of high school. The SAT and ACT are required exams for entrance to most selective universities. Statistically speaking, more students submit their SAT than ACT scores, but both exams are equally well regarded in the college admissions process.

Many students believe that colleges prefer one exam over another. Marlyn McGrath Lewis, director of admissions at Harvard College, explained that Harvard does not prefer one exam over another by saying that the decision of which exam to take " has the feeling of being a significant choice, fraught with implication, but I do not think it does matter."[43] Looking at the data for Ivy League schools, you'll also see that more admitted applicants submit SAT scores than they do ACT scores.[44] However, this trend seems to be evening out. For example, with Cornell University's class of 2018, 79.7 percent

---

43   Heimbach, Alex. "What Do Ivy League Schools Think of the ACT? *PrepScholar*. March 15, 2018.

44   Ibid.

submitted SAT scores, while only 41.4 percent submitted ACT scores. Yet, for the Class of 2021, 63.7 percent submitted SAT scores and 55.9 percent submitted ACT scores.[45]

Here are some things to consider when deciding whether to take and submit either the SAT or the ACT:

1. You will want to take official practice tests for both the SAT and ACT. Both exams take about three hours to complete. Some colleges no longer require the writing portion, while others still review the writing portion, so be sure to verify that for the colleges on your list.

2. Superscoring is the act of taking a test multiple times and then only submitting your best scores in each subject area to colleges. The ACT offers more opportunities to superscore your exam than the SAT.

3. If you are comfortable with science questions and analyzing data trends, you will be able to do well on the ACT science section.

4. If you need a calculator to answer math questions, you will be more comfortable taking the ACT for the math section, as you can use your calculator for the ACT but not on the no-calculator math section of the SAT.

Bottom Line: A big myth suggests that highly selective universities prefer the SAT over the ACT. Both standardized tests

---

45   Ibid.

are accepted by all accredited US colleges. The admissions committee will honor both tests, so choose the examination you feel the most comfortable taking based on your results from official practice tests. You'll need to prepare for these exams well in advance of taking them—most experts recommend at least one year. Be sure to look at schools' policies regarding testing, because some schools have score choice and others do not. With score choice schools, you can submit only the scores you like, which helps you focus on certain sections and take the test as many times as you would like until you get the best score in each category. Other schools are not score choice and ask that you submit all the scores for each examination you have taken. Those schools tend to look down upon students who take the exam more than three times. So, you have to give each section your best shot every single time.

SECTION 14: SHOULD I SUBMIT ADDITIONAL TEST SCORES OTHER THAN THE SAT OR ACT?

Myth: I do not need to submit more than the required test scores.

Truth: While schools typically want you to submit the test scores for the SAT and/or ACT, if you scored particularly well on subject-specific SAT, AP, or IB tests, you should feel free to share those scores as well. They can only help if the scores are good enough.

See if the school you are applying to is a score choice or non-score choice school. Score choice schools let you submit only your best test scores, whereas schools that are not score choice prevent you from doing so. Make a spreadsheet for the colleges you are applying to and check to see if those schools have score choice policies for certain examinations.

One exam I highly suggest for students to take are SAT Subject Tests. If you are a homeschooled applicant or someone who takes courses online in high school, these tests give admissions officers a sense of your academic abilities in a particular subject area. An SAT Subject Test is a one-hour test that focuses on subjects like history, mathematics, science, or foreign languages. Getting a score of 700 and above will look particularly good.

Dakotah Eddy, former admissions ambassador at Cornell University, said there are a "few reasons that you might want to take a Subject Test. One reason is that top schools require the Subject Tests, because they want a broader range of scores from you."[46] Another reason you want to take SAT Subject Test is to stand out as an applicant. Because a lot of schools do not require Subject Tests, you might want to take them to show you are really interested and have another dimension to your application that they can evaluate you on. [47]

When taking these exams, you want to play to your strengths. If you are a science aficionado, you can take a SAT Subject Test in biology or chemistry. If you are passionate about languages or international relations, you can take an SAT Subject

---

46 Veritas Prep College, "Why You Should Take SAT Subject Tests?" March 15, 2016, video, 2:47.

47 Ibid.

Test in French, Spanish, or Latin, for example. If you speak English as your second language, you might want to show and play up your strengths by taking the English Language and Literature test. You have over twenty tests to choose from, so you can really show your strengths both on an academic and personal level.

In addition, AP scores of 4 or 5 work in your favor. Stephen Pultz, assistant vice president for enrollment at the University of San Diego, said his colleagues find AP courses helpful in evaluating candidates. But he said honors and International Baccalaureate courses can be equally helpful.[48] These scores can also differentiate you from other competitive folks in the pool. Similarly, low AP scores can be a red flag to selective institutions. Do not submit your AP scores if they are low. That will show a discrepancy between your grades in AP classes and your testing abilities, indicating to colleges that your high school inflates the grades of students.

The best time to take these exams is the end of junior year, when you will take most of your rigorous coursework and the core classes will still be on your mind.

Bottom Line: Submitting additional test scores may work well on your behalf. Also, for schools going test-optional, this does not mean that strong scores will not help your application. High scores on standardized tests validate the rigor of your high school's curriculum. If sending your test scores presents a financial burden for you, schools

---

48 Scott Jaschik, "Does AP Still Have Admissions Cachet?" *Inside Higher Education*, June 25, 2018

may ask you to self-report your scores via a PDF document for SAT Subject Test and AP scores, and then you are required to send the official test scores after you are admitted. Having your guidance counselor send them to the school is helpful, since test scores received from guidance counselors are typically seen as official documents. You want to prove that you can succeed in an academically rigorous environment. For some schools, you may even be able to get college credit or higher placement in classes based on those scores.

SECTION 15: WHAT ARE COMMON THINGS TO AVOID WHEN SUBMITTING YOUR APPLICATION?

> **Myth:** If I make an error when submitting my application, my chances of admission decrease significantly.

Truth: Well, it depends on the error, but typically you are not the only one making that error. Applying to college can be a stressful process for students.

College admissions officers are reading these applications really quickly, so they might not notice the typo you are really worried about. "As an admissions evaluator at Brown, we really had to keep up a rigorous reading pace with the regular decision applicant pool, whereby we were expected to read five applications per hour, which equates to twelve minutes per application," said Erica Curtis. "In those twelve minutes, I reviewed the application, standardized test scores, the transcript, the personal statement, and multiple supplemental essays—all while taking notes and making a decision on the admissibility of the applicant."[49]

College admissions officers know you are juggling academics, athletics, social events, and college applications simultaneously. Most mistakes you will never have to worry about, but here are five common errors you can avoid in the application process:

1. Name-switching typos

You should always start from scratch when writing your applications for each college. I've seen countless incidents of students writing, "Harvard is my first-choice school" when applying to Georgetown University. If you find this error, just correct it and send the revised essay to the admissions staff.

2. Negative interactions

You should never send rude messages in writing while communicating with colleges. Many schools track your interactions with all staff on your application folder. Admissions officers are always taking notes, so be nice to everyone you meet.

3. Providing false information

During my time in admissions, I saw students lie about being president of a certain club at their high schools, misrepresent

---

49   Joel Butterfly, "7 admissions officers share the things they never tell applicants," *Business Insider*, February 7, 2018.

their parents' level of education on their application, and provide false information about their participation in athletic sports, in hopes of gaining an edge in the process. The college admissions world is very small. Do not risk getting rejected from all the schools on your college list because you provided false information on your application.

4. Too much parental involvement

Incidents have occurred in which parents call an admissions office and accidentally admit they submitted the application on behalf on their child. We could also always tell if an applicant asked their parent to fill out the application, because they typically listed their date of birth on the application instead of their child's date of birth by accident. The college application process should be about the student. Parents can provide advice, but students should be initiating all communication with the admissions office.

5. Submitting more than is required

College admissions officers have a lot to read. You should be sending only the required materials with optional supplementary materials. Do not send too many extra items that do not add value to your application.

Bottom Line: You must proofread your application before submitting it. But if you happen to submit an application with typos or errors, you can always fix those errors. Most schools have a form typically called an application change form that helps you change errors you may notice after the fact. Also, remember that most admissions officers are spending less than ten minutes reading the application file, so if the typo is small, it might not be worth pointing out, because quite frankly, they might not even notice it. But if the mistake is more egregious, such as if you wrote "Stanford University" where you meant to write "Georgetown University," then resubmitting that essay is worth your time. As always, consult with your school guidance counselor about any changes you would like to make on your application, because they might be able to tell you if that change is necessary and point you in the right direction.

CHAPTER 4

KNOWLEDGE IS POWER

SECTION 16: HOW DO ADMISSIONS OFFICERS EVALUATE HIGH SCHOOL TRANSCRIPTS?

> **Myth:** If I do not take all the honors and AP classes available to me at my high school, I will be at a disadvantage in the college selection process.

Truth: While selective colleges prefer students who take the most rigorous courses available to them in their high schools, they also want students to have a balanced schedule and refrain from overwhelming themselves during their high school years.

"What I tell students, and my own kids, is that you don't have to take every advanced class," says Stuart Schmill, dean of admissions at the Massachusetts Institute of Technology. "My high school daughter, for example, is taking advanced math and science courses but chose not to take advanced English and history."[50]

Since students have a wide variety of curricular options depending on whether they attend a public, charter, private, or nontraditional high school, admissions officers look for rigor in the context of your local high school when evaluating the high school transcript.

When guidance counselors submit transcripts, they also send a school profile. A school profile provides context for evaluating the transcripts. It lists total enrollment information per grade, the mission and vision of the high school, the core curriculum per grade, the admissions process for getting admitted to that high school, average standardized test scores, whether the high school ranks students, and the percentage of all students who are on free or reduced lunch. It also lists the grading system, college matriculation lists for students, and the percentage of all graduates from that school who go on to attend four-year colleges.

When evaluating an applicant's high school transcript, admissions officers first read the school profile to get a sense of that school environment and the opportunities it has to offer students, and then from that initial review, they look at the applicant's transcript to see, based on the programs offered at their high school, which courses the applicant decided to take and how well they did in those courses.

---

50 Jennifer Wallace and Lisa Heffernan, "Advice College Admissions Officers Give Their Own Kids," *The New York Times*, March 17, 2016.

During my time in admissions, students often thought they were at a disadvantage if they took honors courses at their public school while their peers took AP courses at the neighborhood's private school. "Oftentimes I find myself trying to talk students off the AP ledge. I see students who are doing all they can to keep up with the work and don't have time to keep up with the learning," said Rick Bischoff, director of admissions at the California Institute of Technology. "We're not counting APs. Has this student taken a rigorous curriculum? Has it prepared them? It's that engagement that's central." [51]

Nowadays, more and more schools have decided to put a cap on the number of honors, Advanced Placement, and International Baccalaureate courses a student can take, in efforts to create a stress-free high school experience for students. Colleges will only evaluate you in the context of what your high school has to offer. If your school only allows two or three honors or AP courses per year, you will not be compared to a student who took seven or eight honors or AP courses because their school allowed them to do so.

When evaluating your application, a college wants to see consistent and upward grade trends, regardless of the course load. Ideally an applicant will have received straight A grades on their transcript for all four years, but colleges understand that extenuating circumstances might affect your academic performance. If your grades during your freshman year were not as great, but you have improved during your sophomore, junior, and senior years, colleges will notice that upward

---

51   Linda Kulman, "How to Get Admissions Officers to Say Yes," *U.S. News & World Report*, August 21, 2008.

grade trend. Conversely, if you start with great grades during your freshman year and your GPA lowers over the next two years, colleges will notice that downward grade trend and it may negatively affect your chances of admissions, unless you have a legitimate excuse for your grades to decline, such as a death in your immediate family or extended illness. If that is the case, you should mention it in your application.

Lastly, colleges want to see that you are consistent with the courses you take. If you take a different foreign language every year since freshman year and apply as a French major or neglect to take a science course for all four years and apply premed, that might negatively affect your chances of admission.

Bottom Line: While you should take rigorous courses to prove to colleges that you are prepared for college-level work, make sure you are leaving time for other things that interest you beside academics. Rest assured knowing that admissions officers do not compare apples and oranges. So be sure to concentrate on what is available to you in the context of your local high school. Before your junior year, you should reach out to colleges to ask questions about which course load is appropriate for you to take to be competitive in the admissions process.

SECTION 17: WHICH EXTRACURRICULAR ACTIVITIES SHOULD I LIST ON MY RÉSUMÉ?

Myth: A long list of activities is what matters most to colleges.

Truth: When deciding on extracurricular activities, focus on depth over breadth by participating in fewer activities that you dedicate more effort toward instead of clubs that you merely signed up for.

Stuart Schmill, MIT dean of admissions, offers high school students this litmus test when choosing extracurricular activities: "If you couldn't write about this on your college application, would you still do it? If the answer is 'no,' then you shouldn't be doing it."[52] He also said, "Applicants do not need to 'tick off' a laundry list of engagement in every field, like art, music, sports, since MIT and other highly selective colleges want students who prioritize quality over quantity."[53]

Admissions officers are interested in what you do outside the classroom. However, do not feel obligated to participate in a long list of activities that you are not interested in doing so you can look impressive to colleges. Like I mentioned in the epigraph, building a class is similar to forming an orchestra, in that orchestras need different instruments and skills to make a beautiful sound. If the orchestra only had principal violin players, it would not work out! In the same way that orchestras need a diverse class of musicians who play different instruments to make a beautiful sound, on college campuses, we want different students with unique skills, talents, and diverse backgrounds to form a vibrant campus community.

---

52 Jennifer Wallace and Lisa Heffernan, "Advice College Admissions Officers Give Their Own Kids," *The New York Times*, March 17, 2016.
53 Ibid.

That is why a college looks for no one particular person when reviewing applications. You are looked at in the context of those around you and how you fit in and work in harmony with other students in the application pools. The honest truth is to do what you are passionate about, because that is what will make you stand out. Also, be sure to include a brief description of the clubs you are involved in at your school. Some college admissions officers might not know whether your high school band consists of three or thirty students, or they might not know whether your debate team has won competitions in the area. You should provide context on the activities and discuss what you have accomplished in detail.

For some applicants, extenuating circumstances might limit your involvement in the extracurricular activities available at your high school. Admissions officers understand that for some families, for either cultural or economic reasons, students have to stay home to babysit or help out with other chores in the house after school.

Moira Poe, associate director of admissions at Yale University, stated that "if you devote a significant amount of time caring for family members, include that, because context is important when we are reading your activities list."[54]

Laura Simmons, assistant director of undergraduate admissions at Georgia Institute of Technology, added that she does not look "for students to have done any particular activity." Instead, she is "looking to see how students grew from

---

54 Yale Undergraduate Admissions, "Admissions Advice: Activities," December 5, 2017, video, 1:53.

whatever they undertook." She said she sees students who are "doing magnificent research" and she also sees students, like her daughter, who are "working as a lifeguard at the pool all summer, and they are both learning from those experiences."[55]

Bottom Line: Admissions officers are interested in what you do outside the classroom. However, do not feel obligated to participate in activities that you are not interested in to look impressive to colleges. Poe said you "should not pursue an activity you don't enjoy, just because you think it might help you get into college." Poe explained, "If that activity isn't meaningful to you, including it in your application will only add clutter, and it might make it more challenging for the admissions officer to understand who you really are."[56] Colleges welcome students with a variety of skills and backgrounds. Sometimes, students only have time to participate in one sport at their school. Other students love engaging with a variety of clubs and developing skills in different areas. While no right list of activities exists, students must ensure they have a well-balanced high school experience.

SECTION 18: HOW CAN I BUILD A BALANCED COLLEGE LIST?

Myth: I should apply to at least twenty colleges if I want to get into one of them.

---

55 Jennifer Wallace and Lisa Heffernan, "Advice College Admissions Officers Give Their Own Kids."

56 Yale Undergraduate Admissions, "Admissions Advice: Activities."

Truth: Although students have no limit to the amount of colleges they may apply to, they should build a balanced college list instead of only applying to the most selective schools. Usually, the average number of schools students apply to is eight to twelve, though this number is rapidly increasing due to stiff competition at the most selective universities.

Before finalizing your list, research different colleges by either visiting campus during the summertime or checking out their website. Look at the different academic offerings, facets of student life, and research opportunities available for undergraduate students to see if that college is a good fit. Be sure to look at the tuition and fees as well as scholarship opportunities to see if you will be able to find financial resources to support your application. Ultimately, you want to find the right "fit" for your personality, needs, and study habits.

Ultimately, your list should make up a combination of "safety," "probable," and "reach" colleges. "Safety" colleges are the schools you have a high chance of gaining acceptance to because you fit the profile for the students they normally accept from your school. You should have at least two safety schools on your list, one for academic safety and one for financial safety.

"Probable" colleges are the ones students would be glad to attend, even if those schools are not your first choice. You fit the general criteria for admission at that school, but there is still a good chance you might not get in. Students should have three to five probable colleges under consideration.

The "reach" colleges are top choices that are highly selective and competitive. You may be a great fit for these universities, but competition is tough for limited first-year spaces. You should have two to four colleges in this category.

Debra Wingood, who worked in admissions at colleges such as Tufts, Georgetown, and Duke, tells students preparing for college applications: "Make an informed forecast by studying the admissions process, the colleges, and, most importantly, yourself." [57] She added that students need to plan on "investing time and effort to seek insight from those you know."[58]

In trying to find your best fit, here are some factors to consider when building your college list:

1. **Size**: Small liberal arts college, such as Amherst College, Swarthmore College, and Washington and Lee University, are known for small class sizes and small student-to-faculty ratios. Medium-sized colleges, such as Villanova University, Duke University, and Georgetown University, are known for manageable class sizes with strong school spirit. Large colleges, such as Virginia Tech and Penn State, are known for big sports cultures and large class sizes.

2. **Distance from home**: You must remember to consider how close you want to be to your home. Although some students want to be as far away as possible from home, others may need to be closer to home for a variety of reasons. You might have a parent who is sick and ailing

---

57   College Board, "How Many Applications Are Enough?" accessed June 4, 2020.

58   Ibid.

or a younger sibling you need to visit often. Colleges have huge out-of-pocket costs, and if you have to take a plane home every time, that mode of transportation is more expensive than being able to take the train home.

3. **Campus type**: Do you want to live in a city, suburb, or rural environment? If you prefer to experience city life while on a college campus, schools like New York University, Columbia University, the University of Pennsylvania, and Georgetown University may be of interest to you. If you prefer to live in a college town in the middle of nowhere, schools like Dartmouth College may intrigue you.

4. **Major**: Transferring into or out of certain majors once you have enrolled in college can be difficult. Spend some time thinking about the academic offerings available at the universities you plan to apply to.

5. **Social life, interests, and vibe**: Is a conservative or liberal environment a good fit for you? Do you want to play club and intramural or Division I sports in college? Do you have a particular interest in singing a cappella, improvisation, or outdoor clubs? Would you like to study abroad during college? Does religious affiliation matter to you?

Gil Villanueva, associate vice president and dean of admission at the University of Richmond, said he encourages prospective students to look at the "three rates" for each college before adding them to their college list.[59] The first is

---

59 Jennifer Wallace and Lisa Heffernan, "Advice College Admissions Officers Give Their Own Kids."

the retention rate: Are students returning as sophomores? Because if they are, you could make the argument that they have had a good experience and their needs are met.[60] Next is the graduation rate—are students graduating on time and within four years?[61] The last rate is the placement rate, which seeks to ask what students are doing six months, a year, or five years after graduation. Are they employed? Are they in graduate school? What type of companies or organizations do they work for?[62]

Bottom Line: Remember to keep an open mind about the college process and do your research when building your college list. It is not about applying to more schools, but applying to a wide range of "safety," "reach," and "probable" schools that will help you gain admittance to at least one school. The United States has over five thousand universities, and more than one school will be a great fit for you. During the summer before senior year, take the time to visit colleges to get an official tour to explore your options. As you visit each college, be sure to keep a journal so you can keep track of where you visited and make note of any initial impressions.

SECTION 19: SHOULD I APPLY EARLY OR REGULAR DECISION?

Myth: Applying early to a school increases my chances of getting in.

---

60 Ibid.
61 Ibid.
62 Ibid.

Truth: While applying early through early decision (ED) and early action (EA) plans may at times be beneficial to applicants, it only truly helps those who have thought through their college options meticulously and have a clear preference for one university.

Many students are told that applying early to your dream college means you will be competing with fewer applicants, which increases your chances for admittance.

Colleges vary in how many students they plan on admitting early and are still competitive regarding the applicants they choose to admit in their early class.

You need to understand the difference between applying "early action" vs. "early decision" to a school. Early action programs are nonbinding, meaning if you are admitted by December, you will have until May 1 to make a final decision. EA is a good option for students who want to receive an early response but not have to commit to the college immediately so they can receive responses from other schools before committing. Typically, if you apply early action, you either get accepted, denied, or deferred. Deferred means the admissions committee has not made a decision on your file and will need more time to think about it.

Early decision plans are more restrictive as they are binding—a student who is accepted to a university as an ED applicant must attend that particular college. The decision rendered by the admissions office is binding if you are admitted.

Here are different scenarios:

If you apply early decision to a college by November 1 and are admitted by December 15, the early release date, then congratulations! You know where you are going to college. Enjoy the rest of your senior year.

If you are deferred during the early process, then you should apply to eight to twelve more schools (refer to the section on Building the College List). Your application is no longer binding. So if you are not admitted early decision to a college because they defer you in December, if that same college accepts you by March, you are not obligated to go there. You will make your decision based on all the other offers you have.

If you are denied admission during the regular process, that is typically the end of the process for that application cycle. You can choose to reapply as a transfer applicant the following year.

Katharine Fretwell, dean of admission and financial aid at Amherst College, said her school and about thirty other universities share lists of students admitted through early decision. She would also share the names of students admitted via early decision, but who are not attending for financial aid and other reasons.[63]

Other schools may not be that strict. "We're not going to come after them," said Mildred Johnson, associate vice provost for enrollment management and director of undergraduate admissions at Virginia Tech, where about twenty-five to thirty students accepted via ED decline the offer each year for a

63 Alexandra Pannoni, "What Happens to Students Who Back Out of Early Decision Offers," *U.S. News & World Report*, October 24, 2016.

variety of reasons. "It's just kind of an honor thing—you said you were going to do this. But no, we are not chasing them down."[64]

If you are considering applying for financial aid and comparing offers among schools, I would highly suggest you do not apply ED. One of the biggest downsides of applying early decision is the disadvantage for low-income and middle-income applicants who could benefit from comparing financial aid offers from a variety of schools before committing to a college.

Athletes are typically encouraged to apply early as well.

Bottom Line: At the majority of schools, students are commonly admitted in the early round, especially nowadays. So, you'll want to check out the early policies for each school. While EA schools tend to be less restrictive, ED policies are binding, which means that if you apply to a school early decision and they accept you, then you must attend that school. However, if you apply ED to a university, be sure it is your first-choice school. Do not try to game the system, because that may backfire. If you betray the binding contract, you may run the risk of getting your acceptance offer rescinded at many schools. If you are applying early to a school, indicate on your application that it is your first-choice school. You do get certain advantages in applying early, especially if you have done your research beforehand and plan on taking all your standardized test before the deadline and want an early answer. While applying early has its

---

64 Ibid.

advantages, make sure you are considering all your options, especially if you are interested in applying for scholarships. Talk to your parents and guidance counselor to discuss what will work for you.

SECTION 20: WHAT DO COLLEGES WANT TO SEE IN MY APPLICATION ESSAYS?

Myth: I need a heart-wrenching sob story to get into college.

Truth: Many students believe that sharing sob stories in their essays will help them get admitted into highly selective colleges, but the truth is that all topics are welcome. Although I have read some heart-warming stories from applicants who grew up with incarcerated parents, endured a mental illness, or dealt with the death of a loved one, you do not need an emotionally wrenching story to get accepted into college. Positive stories are welcome as well. If you went on an amazing trip abroad with your family or started a club at your local high school, you are encouraged to write about that as well. The most important thing is that you are reflective and tell the admissions officer something they would not find out about you anywhere else on the application. Be mindful to not paraphrase parts of your résumé in the college essay.

The most important thing about the essay is writing honestly about something important to you. Start early and get someone to read several drafts of your essay. Your best friend should be able to read the essay and see your personality reflected in it. Lastly, do not forget to spell-check.

Here is what other admissions officers from selective colleges have to say about the essay portion:

1. Shawn Felton, Director of Undergraduate Admissions, Cornell University

"Remember to respond to the question in the prompt and answer the question. Since so many students do not do that, you can stand out by actually answering the question."[65]

2. Jan Deike, Assistant Director of Admissions, Vanderbilt University

"Sometimes students feel that because they haven't found the cure for cancer, they have nothing to share. Life is truly lived in the smaller moments, and that can be a powerful essay."[66]

3. Lorenzo Gamboa, Senior Associate Director of Admissions, Santa Clara University

"Students do not need to compile an entire season into an essay. Just give us one place, one time, one moment, and that will do it for you. The key is to show genuine passion, commitment, and that they have what it takes to survive at the school."[67]

---

65 WowWritingWorkshop, "Tips from the College Admissions Office: Cornell University," October 21, 2013, video, 2:44.

66 Kim Lifton, "College Essay Tips from the Admissions Office for your students," LINK for Counselors, 2020.

67 Ibid.

4. Angela Dunnham, Former Assistant Director of Admissions, Dartmouth College

"As an admissions officer, I analyzed students' personalities. If I read an admissions essay and the student came off as arrogant, entitled, mean, selfish, or, on the flip side, funny, charming, generous, witty, I wrote that exact trait in my notes. It's not enough just to be smart at top schools. Students must also show that they'll be good classmates and community-builders."[68]

5. Calvin Wise, Director of Recruitment, Johns Hopkins University

"I never run into a colleague's office and say, 'Look at this 4.0 GPA.' I will run into an office with a good essay to share; that excites me."[69]

6. Stephen Farmer, Vice Provost for Enrollment and Undergraduate Admissions, University of North Carolina, Chapel Hill

"My advice to students is to first show your essay to a friend and ask, 'Can you hear my voice in this? Could you pick my essay from a stack of two hundred?' The essay doesn't have to be about something life-changing or confessional. Smaller topics, written well, almost always work best."[70]

---

68 Joel Butterfly, "7 admissions officers share the things they never tell applicants."

69 Kim Lifton, "College Essay Tips from the Admissions Office for your students."

70 Jennifer Wallace and Lisa Heffernan, "Advice College Admissions Officers Give Their Own Kids."

7. Stuart Schmill, Dean of Admissions, Massachusetts Institute of Technology

"One of the mistakes students make is that they don't answer the question we ask. They have some essay they wrote for some other school and they try to fit that into one of our questions. That tends not to work, because then we're not learning what we're trying to learn about them."[71]

Bottom Line: The college essay is one portion of the application that is completely within your control. Because the application process, in general, is largely impersonal, what you say in the college essay portion and how you say it are extremely important for standing out in a competitive pool. Your college essay is a great opportunity to reveal who you truly are and to show the admissions committee what makes you unique. If you have the opportunity to visit the colleges, ask the college representative about the role the essay plays at their respective school. During my time in admissions at Georgetown, I saw the college essay was important to reflect the major the student applied for. We were typically looking for programmatic fit and wanted to see that the applicant had researched Georgetown's program offerings within the different majors available. When writing your college essays, please tailor it to each school. Admissions officers can tell when you submit an essay you have written for another school versus an essay you wrote for that specific school. When writing this essay, remember to focus on answering the prompt and telling your story in the most authentic way possible without regurgitating your résumé.

---

71   Ibid.

CHAPTER 5

EMBRACE WHAT MAKES YOU UNIQUE

———

SECTION 21: HOW DO I APPLY TO COLLEGE AS A HOMESCHOOLER?

> **Myth:** College admissions officers do not believe homeschooled applicants are as qualified for admission at a selective university.

Truth: Well, it depends on the rigor of your homeschool education. Many elite universities state that they do not evaluate homeschooled applicants differently than others in the admissions process. Although few publicized statistics exist on the percentage of homeschooled applicants accepted into elite universities, still a sizable portion of that population finds a way to be competitive in the college admissions process.

"It's really important that a home-schooled student shares with us a really detailed account as to how they came to be a home-schooled student and what they've done with their time as one," said Brittney Dorow, assistant dean of admission at Colgate University, "and that's going to come in a transcript that they have written out, which will detail a trajectory as well as the classes that they've taken and give an explanation of what those courses are."[72]

As a homeschooled student, you should be asking: How can I most clearly communicate to the admissions office what I have accomplished and what I am capable of contributing academically and socially to a campus environment? Here are some things you can do to stand out in the admissions process as a homeschooled applicant:

1. **Take courses at a community college.** I would advise homeschooled students to take dual enrollment courses at a local community college. Admissions officers want to know how well you will succeed in an academic environment in collaboration with other students. While it is great that you are excelling in your homeschool courses, taking courses at a community college, especially one of the five core classes like mathematics, English, history, science, or foreign languages, adds credibility to your application. In addition, you will be able to get college credit for those courses, and those instructors can provide you with recommendation letters as well.

2. **Be sure to include a detailed description of coursework.** Usually traditional students' guidance offices

---

72 Allison Slater Tate, "Colleges Welcome Growing Number of Homeschooled Students," *NBC News*, February 17, 2016.

provide a school profile that gives colleges general information about the student body and courses available to students at that specific high school. Homeschooled applicants will need to do that for themselves. They will need to list out specific curricula used and write at least a paragraph detailing what was learned in each class. You might benefit from a narrative transcript. A helpful tool you should use to create the transcript is the website called transcriptmaker.com. Transcript Maker is beneficial for homeschoolers. It is a fairly inexpensive service that helps you create a professional transcript in no time.

3. **Take the standardized tests, even if the school is test optional.** While some schools have test-optional policies, they usually want to see the scores from standardized tests for homeschooled students. Remember that you are going to be competing with students who have followed a more traditional path that colleges are already familiar with. The more you can do to demonstrate that the nontraditional path to schooling you took is rigorous, the more credibility your application will have.

Also, feel free to submit extra letters of recommendation to strengthen your candidacy. Although I would not recommend this for students from traditional schools, extra recommendations can be especially helpful for many homeschooled applicants. Homeschooled applicants tend to have "thicker folders, in a good way," Amherst College Dean of Admission and Financial Aid Katie Fretwell told *NBC News*. "They can be innovative thinkers with a lot to bring to the table."[73] Although colleges welcome recommendation letters from parents, colleges want you to submit at least three other recommendation letters but no more than five from people who are not family members, such as coaches, mentors, job supervisors, clergy, or other teachers.

Interviews are another great way for homeschooled students to stand out. Mary Chase from Creighton University has stated that the "biggest concern for a homeschooled student is often understanding what they're able to do academically but also socially since we want to make sure they're going to fit in."[74] By your scheduling the interview and getting a good report, colleges will be able to gauge how socially adept you are and will be as a student at that university.

Bottom Line: Homeschooled applicants are welcomed in the college admissions process and evaluated with the same regard as other students. You just need to demonstrate that what you have done works outside the traditional scope of schooling in a way that impresses the admission staff in an increasingly competitive world. Make sure that if you're taking online classes, your school is then accredited. Ask each college their policies and how they read homeschooled applicants in their application pool. Visit every school on your list and talk to as many people on campus as possible. If you know other homeschooled applicants who were successful in getting into their dream school, get in touch with them for advice as well.

---

73   Ibid.

74   Robin Mamlet and Christine VanDeVelde, *College Admission: From Application to Acceptance, Step by Step,* (New York: Three Rivers Press, 2011), 344.

SECTION 22: HOW DO I APPLY TO COLLEGE WITH LEGACY STATUS?

> **Myth:** If I have legacy status at a college, then I can bet I will be admitted there.

Truth: Generally speaking, while applicants who are considered "legacy" to the college are admitted at a higher rate on average than those without the "legacy" affiliation, students who receive the legacy tip still have to fill out the same application and be competitive to get accepted. Having legacy status is far from a guarantor of admission to the college. As they used to say in the admissions world, "Legacy status can cure the sick, but it can't raise the dead."

Admission "tips" are special considerations given to students who meet an institutional priority. These tips typically go to students with legacy status or great athletic ability.

You may be wondering what constitutes "legacy" for college admissions. A legacy applicant is someone related to an alumnus or alumna of the college either as their child or as a sibling. So, typically, if the person who graduated is your mother, father, brother, or sister, you count as a "legacy" of that institution. Grandmothers and grandparents only count in some instances. While professional degrees (such as graduate studies) at the university are great, they are less likely to get you the legacy tip in the undergraduate admissions process.

Naturally, legacy admission is a consideration in the first place for many reasons. In July 2019, Harvard's new president, Lawrence Bacow, said many legacy applicants are already in the most desirable applicant position. "Their applications tend to be well put-together," Bacow said. "They have deep knowledge of the institution. So, it's a self-selected pool, which, as a group, by almost any metric, looks very, very good relative to the broader applicant pool."[75]

Students who receive the legacy tip will still need to be competitive to gain admittance. Former Stanford University President John Hennessy once said, "We admit one out of every seventeen students who apply. For alumni children, even though the admissions rate for them is two or three times higher than the general population, it's still very tough to get in. The competition is just brutal."[76]

"Every year, around two thousand legacy students apply to Cornell," according to Locke, Cornell admissions officer.[77] He added that most of them are rejected, and a large portion of those admitted are selected through early decision, which he described as the result of a mutual commitment relationship.[78] Be sure to check each school's policy about legacy admissions. Some schools exclusively add the legacy "tip" at only one point in the admissions cycle. For instance, Georgetown University explicitly says they do not give preference to legacies during the early round. The tip is only added during the regular decision cycle.

75 Melissa Korn, "How Much Does Being a Legacy Help Your College Admissions Odds?" *The Wall Street Journal,* July 9, 2018.
76 Stanford University, "Thinking Bigger, Little by Little," *Stanford Magazine,* September/October 2013.
77 Ibid.
78 Ibid.

So, if you applied early, you could not use the legacy tip to get in. Other schools, like Cornell, explicitly ask legacy applicants to apply early if they want the tip to count. "If you really want us to show some commitment to you as a legacy candidate, we want you to show some commitment to Cornell, which means applying Early Decision," Locke said.[79]

Bottom Line: Essentially, while having legacy at your dream school may help you get in, legacy applicants still need to do the work to gain admittance. At most schools, legacy applicants are considered those who have a mother, father, sibling, or grandparent who attended that school. Typically, their families have held longstanding ties to that college by donating over time and volunteering their skills and expertise as alumni. Colleges sometimes acknowledge the work alumni have done for the university by giving their children some preference in the admissions process. As competition stiffens, it becomes more difficult for legacy applicants to get in, especially if they do not have the right credentials for admission. So, if you are a legacy applicant, you must show you really want to go to that university and that you are not being forced to do so by your parents or siblings. Always be the first one to reach out to university admissions officers in your correspondence with them. Do not leave it to anyone else.

---

79   Ibid.

SECTION 23: HOW DO I APPLY TO COLLEGE AS A FIRST-GENERATION COLLEGE STUDENT?

Myth: Being a first-generation college student will place me at a disadvantage in the college admissions process.

Truth: While the application process is tougher to navigate as a first-generation student, that status certainly does not put you at a disadvantage in terms of getting accepted to a selective university.

According to the Department of Education, "first-generation students" refers to those enrolled in postsecondary education whose parents had not attended college.[80] Each school has its own definition of what it considers "first-generation," so you should understand each college's policy on this matter. For example, if your parent completed some college or has an associate's degree, you are still considered first-generation to four-year college admissions officers. Roughly 60 percent of admissions officers said they are likely to increase their recruiting of first-generation students.[81]

When applying to schools, do not leave the section asking for your parents' occupations blank. Some students feel ashamed

---

80 Jeremy Redford and Kathleen Mulvaney Hoyer, "First-Generation and Continuing-Generation College Students: A Comparison of High School and Postsecondary Experiences," *US Department of Education*, September 2017.

81 Rochelle Sharpe, "Are You First Gen? Depends on Who's Asking," *The New York Times*, November 3, 2017.

or choose to omit that information on their application and they miss out on some scholarship opportunities that may arise. For instance, Georgetown University has a program called the Community Scholars Program, which provides a summer immersion program before the start of freshman year and a monetary scholarship for first-generation students. Applicants cannot apply for that; they are nominated internally by Georgetown's admissions office based on what they put on the application. Other schools have programs as well, such as the First Year Student Enrichment Program at Dartmouth College and the First Generation Project at MIT.

You need to disclose that information because it is helpful in providing context to the admissions staff during admissions review. Many universities conduct a "holistic review" of applicants, which takes into account a variety of important factors beyond GPA and standardized testing. This type of review includes consideration for any special situations or obstacles that students may face in their lives. Thus, knowing parents' occupations gives useful context about your upbringing.

On the Common App, use the additional information section to discuss what attending college means for you as a first-generation applicant. Christian West, University of Virginia alum and admissions officer, stated, "High-performing, first-generation, or low-income students often underestimate the reach of their college options."[82] Seek advice from your guidance counselor or community-based organizations so you are not underestimating your strengths in the admissions process. If

---

82 University of Virginia, "UVA Advice from a First-Generation College Student," video, 0:51, December 14, 2017.

you are seeking financial assistance to make college a reality, be sure to fill out the FAFSA application and CSS Profile by the deadline. You might want to consider applying for scholarships geared toward first-generation college students such as the Jack Kent Cooke Scholarship, Questbridge, or the Gates Millennium Scholarship.

Bottom Line: Colleges welcome students from different backgrounds, and that includes first-generation applicants. If you are first-generation, do not doubt your ability to impress a college's admissions committee and showcase what makes you unique, as that is truly what colleges want to see in your application.

SECTION 24: HOW DO I APPLY TO COLLEGE AS AN UNDOCUMENTED STUDENT?

Myth: Undocumented students cannot legally attend college in the United States.

Truth: Many people believe undocumented students are not legally able to attend college in the United States. Although doing so is not easy, undocumented students are, in fact, legally permitted to attend college in the United States, as no federal or state law prohibits undocumented immigrants from attending either public or private colleges in the United States.

An estimated sixty-five thousand children born abroad who are not US citizens or legal residents graduate from US high schools each year.[83] For the purpose of this book, an undocumented student is defined as someone who lives and has attended high school in the United States but does not have official legal status as a citizen, permanent, or temporary legal resident.

"Some schools will treat undocumented students like domestic applicants, meaning they'll consider them with the same financial aid policies as they do for US citizens," said Joel Hart, associate dean of admissions at Pomona College in Claremont, California. "Most schools, however, will treat undocumented students as international students, meaning they'll be competing for more limited financial aid dollars," he added.[84] Students should contact every school on their list to learn the context in which their application will be treated.

Also, colleges really care about maintaining the privacy of applicants during the admissions process. They will never reveal your private information or citizenship status (or the lack thereof) to government officials.

The most stressful part of applying to college as an undocumented student is the financial cost you must bear to complete your education. The best time to start looking for scholarships is junior year. That will give you enough time to talk to others and accept the money you need to finance your education. One way students who are undocumented can

---

83   College Board, "Advising Undocumented Students," College Board Education Professionals, accessed April 23, 2020.

84   Alexandra Rice and Anna Helhoski, "How DACA Students Can Apply to College," NerdWallet, November 9, 2018.

learn more about how to navigate college is through college access programs in their neighborhood. These programs hire staff who understand the needs, concerns, and desires of students with undocumented statuses and can carefully guide you step by step through the process while keeping your privacy rights intact. For example, Golden Door Scholars, a nonprofit based in the greater Charlotte, North Carolina area, announced it will award college scholarships to high-achieving undocumented students without DACA (the Deferred Action for Childhood Arrivals program).

An issue in state education policy is the fact that some state universities make undocumented students who are longtime residents of that state pay the out-of-state tuition fees, which can put college out of reach financially for many students. "Many undocumented students assume—and perhaps are even advised—that they are not eligible for federal financial aid," Melissa Quan, associate director of Fairfield University's Center for Faith and Public Life in Connecticut said. "However, this is not true in all cases. For students with DACA status, completing the FAFSA form or the CSS Profile can help them gather the information needed to apply for other forms of financial aid for which they are eligible."[85] For more information about applying for financial aid, please read the last two chapters of this book.

Bottom Line: If you are an undocumented student, feel free to embrace who you are and your identity in the application process as you see fit. Generally speaking, you can rest assured that admissions officers will keep your status confidential so

---

85   Ibid.

you may feel comfortable writing to them. Colleges find value in bringing your experiences and background to the campus community. Always answer the question about your citizenship status honestly when applying to college. Also, do not be afraid to apply for financial aid. Some states allow students with undocumented status to qualify for in-state tuition, and other states allow for state-run financial aid funds to be directed to undocumented students, especially for students under DACA. Even after you fill out the FAFSA and CSS Profile, be sure to contact the school you are admitted to and figure out the contact information for your direct financial aid supervisor. This person will be able to help you understand your financial aid packages and make the necessary adjustments so you can afford college.

SECTION 25: HOW DO I APPLY TO COLLEGE AS AN LGBTQ STUDENT?

> **Myth:** I should not include my LGBTQ status on my application for fear of being rejected.

Truth: An increasing amount of colleges are asking questions regarding sexual orientation to their undergraduate applicants to make sure they are building inclusive communities. Typically, colleges are asking these questions so they can send admitted students who identify as LGBTQ support services documents along with their admissions letter. "It's not any more intrusive than that," said Michael Barron, admissions director of the University of Iowa.[86]

---

86 Samatha Stainburn, "The Gay Question: Check One," *The New York Times,* July 30, 2013.

Harvard Dean of Admissions and Financial Aid William R. Fitzsimmons told the university's student newspaper that, while identification as LGBTQ does not add a positive "tip" in the application process, Harvard asks that question because they "want to send a positive signal to students who are grappling with the issue of [sexual orientation] or gender identity."[87]

Steps are taken to protect the privacy of the LGBTQ students who are putting themselves out there, so you should not be afraid that colleges will disclose information about you without your permission.

As you visit colleges, here are some things to look for:

1. **LGBTQ resource center**: Some universities have established offices on campus that commit resources to queer-identifying students. Ask if the campus you are visiting has one of these centers.

2. **LGBTQ/queer studies academic major or minor**: More universities are incorporating academic majors in LGBTQ/queer studies that look at the academic theories behind queer identification. Ask if the campus you are visiting offers these programs. You may also want to know if the school has classes that cater to this subject, even if it does not have an official major or minor.

3. **LGBTQ club on campus**: LGBTQ student organizations provide the social setting you might be looking for on

---

87   Justin C. Worland, "LGBT Question May Be Added to Admissions Application," *The Harvard Crimson*, November 16, 2011.

a campus. Remember that college is not only about the academics but also the social networks you will develop.

4. **LGBTQ inclusive policies**: Ask for a copy of the student handbook and look for policies the school has in place that make it LGBTQ-friendly. This information is important because it might also affect your health benefits as a student on campus.

Bottom line: You should feel free to share your LGBTQ identity with colleges if you feel that it is a significant part of yourself. Colleges are looking to bring all kinds of students to their campus community. They also have policies in place to protect your identity. So feel free to bring your authentic self to the table. Christoph Guttentag, who is Duke's dean of admissions and has read more than fifty thousand essays, said that "when students present themselves as who they are, it's rewarded in the admissions process. Authenticity is perhaps the attribute we see too rarely."[88] As you start building your college list junior and senior year, you should attend LGBTQ college fairs that identify universities with LGBTQ-friendly policies, as you want to spend the four years in college at a place that will embrace your identity and pair you with like-minded peers.

---

88 Steven Petrow, "Should a Student Conceal Her Lesbian Identity in College Application Essays?" *The New York Times*, December 3, 2013.

CHAPTER 6

UNDERSTAND THE PROCESS

SECTION 26: DOES GEOGRAPHY MATTER IN THE ADMISSIONS PROCESS?

> **Myth:** The location where you live does not matter to college admissions officers.

Truth: Colleges are looking to increase diversity in their student body. While racial and socioeconomic diversity is important, most people do not consider how geographic diversity plays a role in the admissions process. "One of the things I half-jokingly tell parents when they ask, 'How can I increase my child's chances?' is 'You should move to Alabama,'" said Irena Smith, a former admissions officer at Stanford University.[89]

---

89 Corinne Purtill, "If you want to get into an elite college, you might consider moving to one of these states," *QUARTZ*, April 4, 2016.

You might be surprised to learn that part of where many students end up going to college depends on where they live. In fact, the majority of incoming freshmen—about 57.4 percent—attending public four-year colleges enroll within fifty miles from their permanent home.[90]

As colleges seek to increase diversity, they have started to look for students who come from diverse locations. "Every school likes to be able to stick that little pin on the map and say they have kids from all fifty states," said Andrea van Niekerk, a college admissions consultant and former associate director of admissions at Brown University. "If you've got two kids and one is from this wacky place—not that Wyoming is a wacky place—that might be the factor."[91]

Christine Chu, former assistant director of undergraduate admissions at Yale and Georgetown, said she "doesn't think colleges lower admissions standards for regional affirmation, but, all things being equal, they may take more top students from top local high schools."[92]

Zach Wielgus, former senior director of undergraduate admissions at Boston College, said the importance of geography in the admissions process varies according to school. "Where

---

90 Nicholas Hillman and Taylor Weichman, *Education Deserts: The Continued Significance of "Place" in the Twenty-First Century. Viewpoints: Voices from the Field*, Washington, DC: American Council on Education, 2016, Page 2.

91 Corinne Purtill, "If you want to get into an elite college, you might consider moving to one of these states."

92 Ilana Kowarski, "How Your Hometown Could Affect Your College Prospects," *U.S. News & World Report*, September 10, 2018.

you live could provide you a small boost in the admission process, or it could be completely irrelevant," he suggested.[93] However, college admissions experts say that while geography is a factor in private undergraduate program admissions, it is not weighed nearly as heavily as academic credentials. They recommend that college applicants focus first and foremost on showcasing their academic promise and their long-term career potential.

Nowadays, many pipeline programs are recruiting students from rural areas, especially Appalachia. These national organizations include Matriculate, the College Advising Corps, and the Rural Pathways Project. Some schools are looking to add to their diversity by recruiting students with a rural perspective.

Bottom Line: Most highly selective colleges care about bringing geographic diversity to their campus. In fact, colleges brag about having as many states and countries as possible represented on campus. Colleges are truly seeking to be global and they want their classes to represent the world. Geographic diversity is not only a great marketing tool for universities, but it also brings different perspectives to their student bodies that serve campus communities well, both inside and outside of the classroom. As an applicant, take advantage of colleges' desire for geographic diversity. Look up the statistics behind the college's geographic diversity, and if you live somewhere colleges are looking to attract more students from, such as a rural community, bring that up in

---

93   Ibid.

your essays. While geography is not the only equation factored in, it can only help you in the admissions process. There are financial implications to going to college in state versus out of state in terms of tuition, so please remember to read the last two chapters in this book, which speak to financial aid and scholarship opportunities.

SECTION 27: WILL ATTENDING A SUMMER PROGRAM AT A UNIVERSITY INCREASE MY CHANCES OF GETTING IN?

> **Myth:** Attending a summer program at a highly selective university will increase my chances of getting into that university.

Truth: When I was in high school, my entire circle of friends applied for the Johns Hopkins Center for Talented Youth summer high school programs. The summer program at Johns Hopkins offers programs to intelligent students in grades seven through twelve the opportunity to take challenging classes on its campus during the summer with other like-minded peers across the nation. I remember being fascinated by the overwhelming interest of my classmates in taking academic courses over the summer. One of my friends boldly stated that she attended Johns Hopkins's CTY program simply because she believed that participating guaranteed admission into Johns Hopkins and other selective colleges.

I later learned that this idea is a huge myth. "The admissions office on a campus is separate from the summer-program office," said Eileen Cunningham Feikens, director of college counseling at the Dwight Englewood School in New Jersey. "The myth out there is that if you attend a particular summer program at a school, then you have a leg up for the admission to that institution."[94] My classmate who participated in the CTY program was not admitted to the Johns Hopkins University for premedical studies. My friend who participated in the Harvard summer program did not get into Harvard, and my other friend who participated in the Columbia summer college program did not get into Columbia University. Though they did end up attending great schools (Yale and the University of Virginia), I realized that while the summer programs were academically enriching, they had little to no bearing on whether the student got acceptance to the school.

"As an educator and a counselor, I do not feel that a student has to do one thing or the other to look good on an application," said Eric J. Furda, dean of admissions at the University of Pennsylvania. "The insights that come from a summer program can help a student later on to tell their authentic story. But, they don't have to be on Penn's campus [or a campus elsewhere] for six weeks to do that," Furda added.[95]

"Going to a certain summer program will not be the tipping point for admission," said Katherine Cohen, founder and CEO of the college counseling firm Ivy Wise.[96]

---

94   Eric Furda, "College Admission: Will the Summer Program Help You?" The University of Pennsylvania, February 23, 2018.

95   Ibid.

96   Laura Reston, "College Summer Programs for High Schoolers: Are They Worth It?" *Forbes*, July 1, 2015.

"The vast majority of the classes are taught by instructors with no connection to the institutions," says Larry Guillemette, chief academic officer for JSA Summer Programs run by Stanford, Georgetown, Princeton, and the University of Virginia.[97]

These programs earn millions of dollars per year for universities and serve as a fundraising arm at times. "For universities struggling to earn back the chunks of their endowments carved out during the recession, those fees are likely quite welcome, bringing in a steady stream of cash during the summer," said Laura Reston, author of *College Summer Programs for High Schoolers: Are They Worth It?*[98]

Although these summer programs may have little to no bearing from an admissions standpoint, they do offer great learning experiences for students and introduce them to life away from home. For some students, this program is the first time they are given the chance to live in a residence hall with others, interact with students from around the world, and learn time management skills.

In the rare case that a summer program helps, it has to be specialized with a niche focus and involve admissions in the process of gaining acceptance to these summer programs. For instance, many selective universities have a goal of increasing the amount of first-generation and low-income students represented on their campus.

---

97 Ibid

98 Ibid.

Bottom Line: "Going to a certain summer program will not be the tipping point for admission," said Katherine Cohen, founder and CEO of the college counseling firm Ivy Wise.[99] While students may feel pressured to attend summer high school programs on college campuses to increase their chances of gaining admittance, admissions officers have said these summer programs rarely give applicants an edge when applying to colleges. If a student got into the university where they did a summer program, they did so on their own merit.

SECTION #28: IS THE ADMISSIONS PROCESS DIFFERENT IF I AM AN INTERNATIONAL STUDENT?

Myth: International applicants to US colleges and universities are considered the same as domestic students.

Truth: While the application process has similar elements for both groups, international students face additional hurdles when applying to US colleges and universities.

The first barrier is that the additional testing requirements for international students can be more of a challenge to gain access to overseas. "One of the most important things for international students is to do their homework early—to make sure they've taken the TOEFL in plenty of time to get the information to the schools they're applying to, and to carefully understand if other test scores are required of

---

99 Ibid.

international students or not," said Pamela Horne, former dean of admissions at Purdue University. [100]

"The way we look at applications is very holistic so all of the pieces are looked at together, but the most important thing that we are going to look at first is the transcript and record of grades at school," said Rebekah Westphal, codirector of international admissions at Yale University. "Students should really be predicted "A" on the A levels examination and mostly six and seven on the IB exams."[101]

Admissions officers know that some scores, such as the International Baccalaureate (IB) results, come after admissions decisions have been rendered. Debra Von Bargen, IB parent and assistant dean of admission at Stanford University, said they still care about the scores even if they come in late. She added that "the colleges to which a student has been admitted and plans to enroll is going to be asking for those diploma scores in the summer."[102] Be sure to not slump academically in the end, because your offer of admission is contingent on academic performance on all grades, including IB examinations.

In addition, financial aid status does play a factor for international students, and most schools are need-aware

---

100 Robin Mamlet and Christine VanDeVelde. *College Admission: From Application to Acceptance, Step by Step.* (New York: Three Rivers Press, 2011), 360.

101 *US-UK Fulbright Commission.* "Application Tips from Yale University." September 19, 2020. video, 10:17.

102 *International Baccalaureate.* "Do IB Diploma scores influence admissions offers at US colleges and universities?" April 18, 2016. video, 1:06.

for international students. Kevin Martin, admissions officer at the University of Texas at Austin, said the reality is that most international students are going to have the money to pay for college, typically the full tuition. But he does offer another approach to minimizing financial expenses for international students by expressing that students can receive a student visa and enroll at a community college for a year or two to establish residency and adjust to the US system before switching to a four-year residential college.[103]

Additional tips from my experience working in admissions include:

1. Find the international admissions representative for your local area.

2. If your transcript is not in English, you need to pay for your transcript to be translated.

3. Make sure to apply early for financial aid. Ask about merit-based scholarships for international students.

4. Work on essays. Your essays will be used to evaluate your ability to write proficiently in English.

5. Keep grades up even after your admissions decisions have been rendered.

---

103 *UT Admissions Guy.* "UT-Austin Admissions Tip #14: International Applicants." July 25, 2016. video, 8:18.

Bottom Line: Overall, colleges want international students to make up a portion of their student body. "Students learn as much from their peers as they do from their professors," explained Kelly Walter of Boston University. Colleges "really want our students to be exposed to opinions of students who come to study here from abroad and who have experienced a very different view of the world than the one our US students might have."[104] So, if you are interested in attending a US-based college as an international student, go for it! If you get the chance to do so, you should visit colleges in the US before applying to get a sense of the campus environment and understanding of what it would be like to attend that college. The earlier you research the US admissions process, the better your application will read to the admissions office.

SECTION 29: WHAT EFFECT DOES INDICATING A MAJOR HAVE ON MY APPLICATION?

> **Myth:** The major of interest I list on my college application does not matter.

Truth: Though you do not have to officially declare a major when you are applying, you should think through what your potential major of interest may be, because at most universities you are applying to a specific college based on your future interest in the majors available at that school.

---

104 Robin Mamlet and Christine VanDeVelde. *College Admission: From Application to Acceptance, Step by Step*. (New York: Three Rivers Press, 2011), 352.

Before you pick an intended major, here are some questions to ask:

1. Is applying to this school more competitive with X major?

2. Is switching majors once I enroll as a student easy?

3. What requirements do I have to complete as part of this major?

At times, the major you list on your application may increase or decrease your chances of admissions depending on the school's priority.

"One thing we always want is humanists," Fitzsimmons said, adding that there were "fewer and fewer" of them.[105]

At Georgetown University, you are applying to one of four undergraduate schools, which include the Georgetown College, the Walsh School of Foreign Service, the McDonough School of Business, and the School of Nursing and Health Studies. When you apply to Georgetown, the major and school you list matter in the admissions process.

However, at Yale University, all applicants submit the same materials and are evaluated through the same processes regardless of their intended major.

So, you may be asking, *How can I narrow down my interests and pick an intended major?*

---

105 Ibid.

If you loved your English classes in high school, think about:

- Comparative literature
- English
- Philosophy
- Communications & technology
- Journalism & media studies

If you love math:

- Accounting
- Business
- Mathematics
- Computer science
- Economics
- Engineering

If you love science:

- Biology
- Chemistry
- Nursing
- Premedical studies
- Environmental or biochemical engineering

If you love history/social sciences:

- Sociology
- Psychology
- Political science
- International relations
- Foreign languages

If you love theater, fine arts, or music:

- Theater/performance studies
- Film/video
- Photography
- Art history
- Dance

After considering the majors listed above, you may be wondering what to do if you are still unclear about your major. If you are undecided, feel free to indicate that as well. You are not alone. "Checking undecided is the most common answer on a college application," said Mary Sue Youn, former admissions officer at Barnard College. "But you want to convey to an admissions office that checking undecided does not mean that you are academically disengaged."[106]

She added that you should look at your academic classes and activities for clues as to what you are interested in. Do you consider yourself a writer? Are you more analytically or quantitatively minded? Do you like hands-on learning experiences? All these questions might be clues as to what a great major for you might be.[107]

Whether you are undecided or considering something really specific like biomedical engineering, please note that your choice is never permanent unless you want it to be. Many students change their majors once they enter college. Studies

---

106 College Coach, "Is it Okay to Apply to College with An Undecided Major?" January 18, 2018, video, 1:57.
107 Ibid.

show that about 75 percent of students will change their minds about what they study upon starting college.

Bottom Line: While some universities do not take intended major into account when making admissions decisions, others require you to have somewhat of an idea of your major in order to choose the undergraduate program you need to apply to for admission. Although this task of narrowing down during your senior year of high school might seem daunting, you can do so even if you are still unclear which profession you intend to pursue. Some schools have opportunities for you to speak to current students as a prospective applicant. You might want to take advantage of that because it will give you insight into what kind of courses that student is taking and how well they enjoy it. Be sure to see what the admissions policy regarding majors is for your school, because most of the time you do not have to commit to your intended major once you are admitted. But some schools require you to take classes in the intended major you listed on your application for at least one year.

SECTION 30: HOW SHOULD I DEAL WITH DISCIPLINARY ISSUES ON MY APPLICATION?

Myth: Omitting information about disciplinary issues that occurred in high school is okay.

Truth: Every college application has a section that asks students to indicate whether they have been found responsible for disciplinary violations in high school. If you have, typically, you're asked to describe what happened and provide dates, as well as a reflection essay on what you learned from that experience. While omitting information about that detention or suspension you received during high school may seem tempting, the truth is that students in high school make mistakes, and if you have made mistakes, this is the time to own up to them and show a college how much you have matured and learned throughout the years.

"To answer 'yes' or not to the question regarding an incident of disciplinary action, suspension, expulsion or conviction of a crime is never easy for a college applicant to do," said Nanette H. Tarbouni, director of admissions at Washington University in St. Louis. "None of us likes to be reminded of our mistakes. It is, however, one of the most important areas of honest communication in the entire application."[108]

"The disciplinary question is not meant to find out all the 'bad' things students have done. Colleges understand that students are people (just like admissions officers), capable of making mistakes or bad judgments. We're not in the business of re-punishing students, either," said Debra Shaver, director of admission at Smith College. "We are, however, in the business of building a community. Most importantly, a community of scholars—but also a community that engages and interacts in a way that is respectful and honorable."[109]

I have been asked whether students should report disciplinary violations when asked on the application, even if such

---

108 "College experts discuss high school suspensions," College Confidential, June 23, 2010.
109 Ibid.

infractions will not show up on the transcripts. The answer is yes. Even if you think that college will not find out about the disciplinary issues, remember that as an applicant, you are not the only one submitting materials, so it might show up somewhere else, such as in the secondary school report submitted by your guidance counselor or in a teacher recommendation.

I have even received phone calls in which administrators from a high school would report the violation without having it in writing on the application. The point is that if you choose not to disclose disciplinary issues on your application, they might show up in another part of the application anyway, which will raise questions about your integrity as an applicant.

"Students and parents should be told that the student must be honest in responding to all questions on a given application," said Pamela T. Horne, assistant to the provost for enrollment management and director of admissions at Michigan State University. "Our question is worded 'have you ever . . .' which means that we do expect a 'yes' response even for 'expunged suspensions.'"[110]

Here are the steps you should take to maintain your integrity, should you have a disciplinary infraction on your high school record:

STEP 1: TELL THE TRUTH.
The first piece of advice is to be as honest and forthcoming possible. Do not feel the need to detail everything that

---

110 Ibid.

happened moment by moment. But be honest about the behavior that took place and the disciplinary action that was enforced. For instance, if you were caught smoking an illegal substance on school grounds, explain that you violated the school's rules or ethics code on substance abuse and had to bear punishment, which resulted in a detention. Remember to be courteous and gracious. Do not try to debate your innocence when writing this report.

STEP 2: EXPLAIN WHAT HAPPENED.

The second piece of advice is to reflect on what you have learned and how you have grown since the incident. This violation is not a scarlet letter, and it will not be held against you forever if you explain how it became a learning experience for you. By showing what you learned from that incident, you have made the admissions committee more sympathetic; your approach comes off as mature.

STEP 3: CONSULT YOUR ADVOCATE.

Remember not to dwell on the fact that you made a mistake. Talk to your guidance counselor on the best way to write the letter for the schools you are applying to. Your guidance counselor is one of your advocates in the process.

Bottom Line: Admissions officers expect applicants to be truthful and honest on their applications. Although applicants have full discretion on what they choose to include or omit in their application, it is in the best interest of the applicant to be forthcoming. During my time in admissions, we admitted students who had disciplinary records and were honest and forthcoming enough to explain what happened and how they grew from that experience. We all make mistakes and should feel comfortable owning up to those mistakes. Since highly selective universities make admissions decisions based on the context of holistic review, if your infraction is minor, it will most likely not affect your chance of admission. If you choose not to report it and it gets revealed somewhere else in the process, your chances of admission at a highly selective university will significantly decrease—so be as honest as possible, because first impressions last.

CHAPTER 7

DO NOT PANIC

SECTION 31: HOW STRICT ARE THE DEADLINES?

> **Myth:** The college application deadline is a strict deadline. If I miss this deadline, I can no longer apply to college that year.

Truth: Well, it depends on what led you to miss the deadline. College application deadlines should be adhered to, but if you have extenuating circumstances that prohibit you from meeting them, do not fret.

Over the past few years, students have missed the application deadlines as a result of natural disasters in the local area, public school turnovers, and sudden death in the family. These circumstances can impact a student's ability to take scheduled standardized tests and submit the required materials on time. For example, in 2019, the number of college applications submitted from California decreased because of a wildfire disaster in the region. As a result, colleges offered students who were affected the opportunity to spend more time completing their applications in light of that situation.

If you do not have a good reason for submitting late, you might be out of luck.

"A simple 'I just forgot,' is not going to cut it," said Jon Frank, founder and CEO of Chicago-based Admissionado. "The last thing you want to do is spend your senior year struggling with the basic task of submitting your application on time due to your own negligence."[111]

Applications typically open during the summertime. While getting ahead of the curve is advantageous, at times you may encounter an earth-shattering incident that disrupts your plans. If you do encounter a situation that prevents you from submitting on time, here are the three steps you should take:

1. Discuss this incident with your high school guidance counselor.

2. Call the admissions office for the school(s) you are applying to and then figure out the contact information for the person you should send the explanation for the late application. Then send that individual a letter explaining why you could not get the application completed on time. If you have contact information from someone you saw during your visit, then contact that person.

111 Caroline Shannon-Karasik. "Did You Miss a College Application Deadline?" Campus Explore, Accessed May 3, 2020.

3. Write an email explaining why you missed the application deadline and discuss what steps you have taken to rectify the error. Be sure to follow up within five days after sending that letter. Be sure that you, as the applicant, are the one who is writing the email and calling the admissions office. Parents calling on behalf of the student sends the wrong message. Cornell B. LeSane II, dean of admissions at Allegheny College, said that you "have to be the driver of the process." He added, "Parents should be a great sounding board, but they should not be the ones filling out the applications."[112]

Note that different types of college application deadlines exist. Here are the different deadlines you may come across when applying to colleges:

1. **Early action deadline**: If you submitted an application to your first-choice college by November 1 and are admitted to that college early, congratulations! You will be given until May 1 to make the final decision. In the meantime, you may choose to apply to a few more colleges if you are unable to get the financial aid package you want from your number-one school.

2. **Early decision round 1 deadline**: If you apply to your first-choice college by November 1 through its early decision program, the school will let you know in December whether you have been admitted. If you get in, you are bound to attend that school. You, your

---

112 Jennifer Wallace and Lisa Heffernan, "Advice College Admissions Officers Give Their Own Kids."

parents, and your guidance counselors will sign an agreement you must abide by. This school must be your first choice, and you must not be concerned about comparing financial aid packages.

3. **Early decision round 2 deadline**: The main difference between the Early decision round 1 deadline and the round 2 deadline is timing. The same rules and regulations apply. If you apply to your first-choice college by January instead of November 1, a college will let you know whether you have been admitted. You are bound to attend that school, if admitted. Typically, students choose this option if they were not admitted early action the first time around.

4. **Regular decision deadline**: This is the most common application deadline, where you apply by late December/ early January and then get a response by mid-March. At most selective colleges, admissions officers do not start reading files until after the regular decision deadline, so there is no need to rush to submit your application early.

5. **Rolling application deadline**: Rolling admissions means the school reviews applications as it receives them. For these schools, no firm deadline exists. You apply with your full application, and between two to seven weeks later you will receive an admissions decision. You will have greater flexibility, but you still need to send in that application as soon as possible.

Bottom Line: Most selective universities have a deadline by which they expect you to submit your application. While adhering to these deadlines is important, if you face a predicament that prohibits you from submitting your application on time, act preemptively and contact your guidance counselor and the admissions officer via the contact information provided by the admissions office. You have two application deadlines to keep in mind when applying to college: *early action* and *early decision* deadlines are set around the beginning of November. *Regular decision* deadlines are set around the beginning of January. Most admissions officers are understanding of extenuating circumstances that prevent you from being able to complete an application on time. Simply let them know ahead of time or include a paragraph with an explanation as to why the application arrived late.

SECTION 32: WHAT SHOULD I DO IF I HAVE MISSING MATERIALS AFTER THE DEADLINE?

Myth: If all the application materials are not in by the deadline, my chances of admission will be negatively affected.

Truth: Nothing comes into the admissions office all at once. Colleges receive thousands of applications via mail and online platforms every year during admissions season that they have to quickly sift through in a short amount of time and place in each applicant's file. Although many colleges are switching to digital online application platforms, many parts of the application, including the guidance counselor letters of recommendation and teacher recommendations, are sent via mail. By the application deadline, they are still in the process of sorting through and filing application documents.

According to Richard H. Shaw, dean of undergraduate admission and financial aid, "A high percentage of our students apply at deadline. So by January 2 we are buried alive in paper, and it stays that way until the end of the month."[113]

If you check your online portal after the deadline and find that one or more of the required documents are not checked off on the list of received items, please do not panic.

"No, you're not in trouble if your materials haven't yet shown up on the tracking system," said Matt McGann, MIT admissions officer. "We're still processing lots and lots of materials, many of which were postmarked before the deadline." Concerning the delays in processing paperwork, he explained that his office is "processing documents from more than ten thousand students, each of whom has multiple letters of recommendation, transcripts, interviews, supplements, test scores, etc. Taken together we will process more than fifty thousand documents over the next few weeks alone."[114]

So, if you receive an email from an admissions office signaling that you are missing materials, here is what you should do:

1. Do not panic! If admissions officers are taking the time to email you about a missing document, they do so because they want you to be able to complete them.

---

113 Elizabeth F. Farrell, "Behind the Scenes, Admissions Offices Conquer Mounds of Mail," *The Chronicle of Higher Education*, January 25, 2008.

114 Chris Peterson, "Missing Documents Due Monday," MIT Admissions, January 26, 2012.

2. Check your application portal to see what is missing.

3. Contact your guidance counselor to help you track down the documents.

4. Send the admissions office an email signaling that you received the missing material email and that you are working on getting the materials in as soon as possible. Remember to be courteous in your email!

5. Submit the materials as soon as possible. Work with your guidance counselor to submit them—the guidance counselor should always be in the loop.

Appropriately filing these documents takes weeks. Once submitted, only call the admissions department to see if the institution has received it after two weeks have passed since submitting the new materials. You may call the school from your school's guidance counseling office so they can confirm the date/time that the missing material reached the admissions office.

If, by chance, you or your guidance counselor did send the missing material and the admissions office still has not received it, then call the office to state when the document was submitted and how it was submitted (via mail or online). At times, the college might say that it is missing a document when it is in the admissions office but has not been entered in the system yet.

Since some colleges are sorting through and filing documents well after the deadline, the missing document is not always missing. Sometimes, it has either been misfiled or is not filed yet. By sending the admissions staff an email stating when you submitted the material, it can usually easily be found.

Most offices do not begin to review applications until at least a week after the deadline, and admissions officers do not make admissions decisions unless they have the necessary information to render a final decision. Nonetheless, you should do your best to submit that missing material within two to five days from receiving the email.

If the school you are applying to uses an online portal, you should ideally submit it through the portal as opposed to by mail. During my time in admissions, I noticed that documents were frequently missing if they were submitted by mail. Otherwise, you may fax the missing documents to your school's office.

Bottom Line: Although students dread receiving a "missing materials" email from their dream schools, please do not panic if you do receive one. During my time in admissions, we wanted to make sure our favorite applicant's file was complete before sending that applicant to committee. While everyone typically tries their best to ensure that all the materials are submitted on time, applicants and guidance counselors can only do so much to ensure that all of the documents required by colleges reach the university on time, if at all. The truth is that you will rarely be penalized for a missing component, especially if it was out of your control. While admissions officers would like to see a completed file for each applicant by the application deadline, we understand that things get lost in the mail, online portals break down around the application portal deadline, and guidance counselors leave their jobs around application time—along with other extenuating circumstances that can result in missing materials. Lastly, please allow for five to seven business days for the admissions office to receive and process the documents before contacting them. Do not feel pressure to submit your application really early, because applications are read after the deadline. Do your best to submit as much as you possibly can and don't panic if you receive a "missing materials" email.

SECTION 33: HOW DO ADMISSIONS COMMITTEES WORK?

Myth: Colleges have only one type of student they are looking to admit.

Truth: Admissions officers read and evaluate applications on a holistic review basis.

Students often think colleges are only looking to admit private school students with a high GPA from a wealthy family with legacy status for that institution. In reality, colleges are looking for many different types of students to bring to their vibrant campus community. When making admissions decisions, colleges are trying to get a sense of not only who you will be in the classroom, but also who you will be as a member of the campus community. To evaluate your application, colleges use holistic admissions factors. Holistic review means that admissions officers will never make admissions decisions on applications based on grades or test scores alone. In fact, James Kim, admissions officer at Yale University, said, "Never let your test scores or your GPA discourage you from applying." He added that in Yale's holistic review process, admissions officers are "looking at every application within the context of that student within the context of their community."[115] He encourages applicants to think about how they can present their narrative in a way that shows admissions officers how they have been able to maximize the opportunities available to them.

Here are the primary factors that admissions officers consider when reviewing your application:

1. **Official transcript**: This document shows all the grades you have received for coursework taken from ninth to twelfth grade. Colleges are looking at the rigor of your curriculum and grade trends over time. Please make sure your guidance counselor also sends in your senior year schedule. Colleges want to see which courses you are taking senior year.

2. **School profile**: Guidance counselors send the school profile to colleges to give them your local school's context. Admissions officers are not able to visit every school. These school profiles help them understand key information about your high school's student body.

3. **Standardized tests**: Typically, colleges require the SAT or ACT examination. They might request SAT Subject Tests and AP exam scores as well.

---

115   Yale Undergraduate Admissions, "Holistic Review," October 28, 2015, video, 2:23.

4. **Extracurricular activities**: Colleges want to see your depth of involvement outside of class—how you spend your time when you are not doing homework.

5. **Essays**: Colleges will typically ask for two essays. Be sure to read the prompts and answer the questions accordingly.

6. **Teacher recommendations**: Choose a teacher who can speak well on your behalf, as colleges take this letter very seriously.

7. **Counselor recommendation**: Be sure to meet with your guidance counselor at least once and provide the counselor with your résumé so they can write you a great letter.

8. **Alumni interview**: This is the only face-to-face opportunity you will have in the admissions process. Be sure to take this part seriously and ask any remaining questions you may have about the school.

Sara Harberson, former admissions officer at the University of Pennsylvania, explained that a tag is the "proverbial golden ticket for a student applying to an elite institution because it identifies a student as a high priority for the institution." She added that "typically students with tags are recruited athletes, children of alumni, children of donors or potential donors, or students who are connected to the well connected."[116]

---

116 Sara Harberson, "Op-Ed: The truth about 'holistic' college admissions," *Los Angeles Times*, June 9, 2015.

These "tags" help students stand out in the applicant pool. Other important "tags" that help students stand out on the application include geographic background, being the first generation in your family to go to college, self-determined identity as a member of an underrepresented minority group, and prestigious awards and honors. As you write your application, tell your narrative in a way that will help you stand out from the crowd, because colleges are looking for many different traits in their applicants based on institutional priorities.

Bottom Line: Holistic review gives the admissions officer a chance to evaluate you by looking at the big picture of who you are as a person and not just as numbers on a page. Everything on the application matters to admissions officers, so you should answer every question to the best of your ability. If the information were not important to the admissions officers, they would not ask it on the application. While you should stay competitive academically, you should also pursue and excel in your passions outside of school. Admissions officers are looking to build a class with students who will complement each other well with their own unique attributes. You are more than your GPA and test scores. Be sure to add context to your application by truly telling your story in the college essay, choosing teachers who know you well to write your recommendation, and taking advantage of the interview process to show that you are passionate and knowledgeable about the schools you have applied to.

SECTION 34: IS APPEALING ADMISSIONS DECISIONS POSSIBLE?

Myth: All admissions decisions are final.

Truth: Although most of the decisions colleges make are final, a few exceptions to the rule always exist. Although appealing a deny decision from college is exceptionally rare, doing so is certainly not impossible. It is common knowledge that few appeals result in an overturned admissions decision, but at least 1 to 2 percent of appeals do work in favor of the applicant.

An appeal for a change in an admissions decision is typically a request for a different decision, based on new information that was not initially shared in your application to college. The new information that would be valid include (1) winning major awards that are academic or athletic in nature, (2) better SAT or ACT test scores than the ones you initially submitted, or (3) a GPA improvement in your final semester of senior year after completing a rigorous course load.

Another issue that is grounds for an appeal is that you have discovered a clerical or procedural error in your application. Did your guidance counselor accidentally submit the wrong transcript on your behalf? Were there courses you took that are not listed on your transcript? Did you upload the accurate senior year course schedule? Was your application incomplete for reasons outside of your control? You will need to be able to document the error, but situations such as these are, in fact, good grounds for appeal. Colleges want to be as fair and equitable as possible in the admissions process. If you were rejected for an error that was outside of your control, colleges will reevaluate their decision.

An appeal should be submitted in writing by the applicant (not an applicant's agent, parent, counselor, or other advocate) and must include the applicant's most recent official transcript. That transcript should be provided directly from your guidance counselor. If you choose to submit an additional letter of recommendation, the committee will review it. However, remember that admissions decisions are not made solely on the basis of an individual letter of recommendation or a specific recommender—so no need to submit more than one additional recommendation letter.

Note that while colleges appreciate the fact that many of their applicants are interested in attending their institution, simply demonstrating interest is typically not the basis for an appeal. The mere act of visiting the campus or submitting an emotional letter or showing interest in other ways does not impact the admission committee's decision. In addition, students must be aware of timelines: "Freshman applicants are given approximately four weeks, while transfer applicants are given two weeks to appeal," said Janet Gilmore from the University of California, Berkeley. "This is in an attempt to complete all releases in a timely manner so students can prepare and plan for their fall terms."[117]

Colleges will review your appeal based on several holistic factors. Some primary consideration factors include:

---

117 Moody, Josh. "A Guide to the College Admissions Appeal Process." *U.S. News & World Report.* March 6, 2020.

1. Academic success in high school

2. Rigorous academic coursework through high school graduation

3. Overall class rank/GPA

4. Those primary consideration factors are within your control. Some secondary review factors include the college's own strategic planning, such as:

5. Enrolling a diverse student body—with students bringing differing experiences, talents, and perspectives to their campus community

6. Strong commitment to community service and leadership

7. Military service

8. Evidence of having overcome social, economic, or physical barriers to educational achievement, such as being a first-generation college student

9. Significant responsibility in a family, community, job, or activity

10. Family employment or family attendance at the university

Bottom Line: You can actually write an appeal letter with the hope that the admissions office will change its decision about your application. Rejection decisions are not always set in stone. Look at the college's policy on appeals. Some universities just do not allow an appeals process. Other universities have rules for such a process. Be sure to contact the admissions office to figure out what the school's policy entails. While asking for an appeal is worth a shot, be prepared to face another rejection decision. At least you'll know for sure you did the best you could do to get accepted.

SECTION 35: WHAT IS THE BEST WAY TO APPROACH THE TRANSFER ADMISSIONS PROCESS?

Myth: I am at a disadvantage if I try to transfer from community college to a four-year college.

Truth: Selective four-year colleges welcome students from a plethora of academic backgrounds. If you are currently attending a college and it is not a good fit, look into transferring.

"A transfer is not a failure," said Carolyn Pippen, former admissions officer at Vanderbilt University." If you decide after your first semester that College A is not for you, take a second look at Colleges B, C, and D. This does *not* mean you failed the first time around, but rather that you are courageous enough to recognize a change needs to be made, and we applaud you for it."[118] It does not matter where you start, but where you end up. In order to get a head start on your application, you should get in touch with the transfer admissions coordinator at the university of your choice to ask questions and get in touch with

---

118   Pippen, Carolyn. "Lessons from a Departing Admissions Counselor." *Vanderbilt University.* May 29, 2014.

current students, preferably those who have been through the transfer process themselves.

Ask these questions on your visit:

- How will the credits I earn transfer at your four-year college?

- Which standardized test should I take to remain competitive in the admissions process?

- What is your cutoff GPA?

- Does my two-year college have a special relationship with your four-year college for preferential admissions?

- Which courses will be accepted for credit as per the school's articulation agreements?

- Have there been any changes to the transfer requirements in the past year?

While most students enter college in the fall, some schools also open their doors to enrollees in the spring semester.

If you are a student athlete, you must follow a few additional rules to transfer. According to the NCAA transfer guide, you can apply for admissions at a new college without notifying the athletics department at your current school, but you have to see if you have continuing eligibility to compete in your sport after transferring to a new school.[119] Be sure to speak to a transfer coordinator who can help you through the process and see if your scholarships will still transfer over or if you need to apply for new scholarships through the school's financial aid process.

Keep in mind that transfer admissions decisions tend to be given out on a rolling basis. If you apply to multiple schools during the transfer process and are admitted to your second-choice school, and your first-choice school has not given you a decision yet, use the admissions offer from your second-choice school as leverage. You should contact the director of transfer admissions of your first-choice school and ask for an early read of your application. Tell them you would really like to transfer to that school, but you have an offer letter from another school that wants you to commit to them in about a week.

Bottom Line: If you are dissatisfied with your current school, you can always transfer to a different college that provides a better fit. Transfer applicants bring valuable experiences and perspectives to the college they will attend. Speak with a counselor to learn the ins and outs of the transfer process at your school. The process is typically similar to the first-year application process, but the deadlines are usually pushed back. Because of the timing of the transfer admissions process, most colleges are unable to consider grades earned in the second semester of the year of your submitted application. If you are applying for sophomore standing, most colleges will only

119 NCAA Eligibility Center, "2018-2019 Guide for Four-Year Transfers: For Student athletes at Four-Year Colleges," accessed June 4, 2020.

receive your first semester grades from freshman year, so try to make sure those grades are an accurate representation of your academic ability. In that case, high school grades and standardized test scores still play an important part of the holistic evaluation of transfer admissions. Note that if you are applying to transfer to a college and have already applied to that college previously, you will need to resubmit your application with new documents, as there is no guarantee the documents you previously provided will roll over.

CHAPTER 8

MAKING THE DECISION: WHAT'S NEXT?

———

SECTION 36: HOW SHOULD I CHOOSE WHICH COLLEGE TO ATTEND?

Myth: Colleges with top ratings in the U.S. News and World Report rankings are the best ones.

Truth: The best college is the one that is the right fit for you. As the May 1 deposit deadline approaches, you may have difficulty deciding which college to attend. When making the decision to attend a college, you must choose the school that is the best fit for your needs. One of the most important ways to do so is to go back to the colleges you were admitted to and attend their accepted student weekends on campus. If you are not able to revisit the campus, you may attend an admitted student reception hosted in your local area. These days, you can even view information sessions and college tours via the college's website or through platforms like Zoom and Skype.

Richard Shaw, Dean of Admissions at Stanford University, once said that in deciding which college to choose, the number one question to ask yourself is, "Where will I be deliriously happy?" If you can answer that question, then that is the answer to the question of where to attend college.[120]

Here are the questions you should consider when making the final decision:

Location:

- Will I be more comfortable attending college in an urban, rural, or suburban environment?

- Do I prefer to dine on or off campus?

- Would I prefer to live on campus or off campus all four years?

- Am I comfortable adjusting to the weather on the East versus West Coast?

- What is the crime rate in the area?

Orientation:

- Will other students from my high school be attending this college?

---

120 *College Admissions*, "Selecting Your College," August 17, 2014, video, 1:21.

- Are there orientation programs available to students over the summer?

- Are there orientation programs available to students on the first week of school?

- Are there ways to connect with students online?

- Will I be able to choose my roommate over the summer?

Academics:

- Will this college accept my AP courses and exam scores as credit?

- When will I have to declare my major?

- Are there opportunities to study abroad?

- Are faculty members available to students?

- What is the average class size for most of the courses?

- Is there a writing center open to undergraduate students?

Extracurricular and social life:

- Are the extracurricular activities student run on campus?

- What clubs are available for undergraduate students?

- Are the clubs competitive or easy to gain access to?

- Can students start their own clubs on campus?

- Is there a club fair for new students? If so, when does it occur?

Career opportunities:

- Will I be able to obtain research assistant positions as an undergraduate student?

- Is the career center readily available to undergraduate students?

- Can I schedule an appointment to meet with a career service representative my freshman year?

- What kind of internship opportunities are available for students in the fall and spring?

- Does this school offer course credit for internships?

Financial cost:

- What percentage of students graduate with student loan debt and how much on average?

- Does financial aid travel with me abroad?

- Does this school offer merit- or need-based financial aid?

- What kinds of work-study opportunities are there? How will I know which ones I qualify for?

Bottom Line: While knowing you have been admitted to college is a relief, narrowing down which school you will attend can be a challenge. By answering these questions, you will at least have an idea of the pros and cons of each campus and narrow down your list to one school. Remember that if you do not end up liking your school of choice, you can always transfer. This is one of the most important decisions you will make in your life, so you should consider your future and be well equipped to make this decision. Many schools offer opportunities to meet with current students or spend a day sitting in classes, so take advantage of those opportunities. Talk to as many people as possible so you can get a sense of the culture of the campus.

SECTION 37: WHAT STEPS SHOULD I TAKE IF I AM PLACED ON THE WAITLIST?

> **Myth:** Getting off the waitlist at my dream school is impossible.

Truth: If you are on the waitlist, that status might feel like "admissions purgatory." You have waited a full year to hear back from your dream school only to hear back that you have to wait for a longer period of time. A waitlist decision may leave you wondering whether you should give up and accept an offer from another school or stick around and hope for the best.

A student is typically placed on the waiting list if they are highly qualified to attend that school but just did not make the initial cut. In my experience in admissions, I have seen students who were waitlisted because no space was left in their intended major. This tends to be more common for students who list "premed," "biology," and "chemistry" as their intended major for college. Most highly selective universities admit knowing that a number of students who were admitted will choose to attend another school. Thus, the waitlist can be seen as the college's safety net, a place where they can go to fill up spots in an incoming class. If you were admitted into some schools but waitlisted at your dream school, you must set up a meeting with your guidance counselor to discuss the situation immediately. Your guidance counselor can serve as a great advocate for you to navigate the waitlist. Admissions officers love to hear from your guidance counselor, especially when considering taking you off the waitlist.

"Some years we've taken zero off the waitlist and some years we've taken more than 100 off the waitlist," admitted Janet Rapelye, dean of admissions at Princeton University. "We asked students when they're on the waitlist to send us updates if they haven't already, but they don't need to send us any new information, since we have everything we need."[121]

If you are on the waitlist of your dream school, don't completely give up! Here are some steps to try to increase your chances of getting off the waitlist.

Step 1: Ask questions.

The first thing I recommend an applicant do if they are waitlisted is call the admissions office and figure out what

---

121 Jordan Goldman, "How can college applicants get accepted off the waitlist?" November 17, 2014, video, 1:24.

percentage of students were pulled off the waitlist from the previous year's application cycle. I would then ask to speak with my regional admissions officer to ask if they believe I have a chance of getting off the waitlist. Also ask the office when they plan on taking students from the waitlist, if at all.

Step 2: Reiterate your interest in attending.

If you still intend on staying on the waitlist, knowing you have a slim chance of being admitted, you should then write to the school in an email to opt in to the waitlist. Each school has its own way of handling the waitlist. Be sure to look up the procedures for individual schools. If possible, write a letter to your regional admissions representative and copy the dean of admissions stating your interest in opting in to the waitlist. In the letter, be sure to include why you would want to enroll at that university and how you see yourself contributing to the campus environment via the courses you plan to take, the professors you plan on meeting/conducting research with, and the activities you plan to participate in.

Step 3: Send updates.

Remember to update the school frequently with any updated information, such as grades, awards, and scores. Talk to your guidance counselor before sending in anything.

Step 4: Avoid senioritis.

Maintain strong senior year grades and keep up a great attitude with your peers, teachers, and guidance counselor.

Step 5: Submit a deposit to another university.

Even if you plan on staying on a waitlist at another school, you should still submit a deposit and plan to enroll at another university. Only send a deposit to one university. Do not fall into the trap of double depositing. Enrollment deposits are usually due by May 1.

Bottom Line: Although being on the waitlist at your dream school is disheartening, you still have hope. Michael Steidel, dean of admission at Carnegie Mellon University, advises students to "examine all of their choices . . . choose the one that's best for them, make that commitment, send an email to the school that waitlisted them and tell them that, if accepted off the waitlist, they will attend . . . and move forward as if [the waitlist] doesn't exist."[122] Once you have had a chance to come to terms with being waitlisted, here are things to know: Colleges usually do not admit from the waiting list until the May 1 decision deadline has passed. Usually, most highly selective universities are committed to removing students off the waitlist by June 30. If you are accepted from the waitlist and decide to attend that college, be aware that the deposit you sent to your alternate college is nonrefundable. If you do not get in off the waitlist, you may reapply the following year as a transfer student.

---

122 Annabelle Timsit, "The case against the college waitlist," *QUARTZ*, March 31, 2019.

SECTION 38: WHAT ARE ETHICAL ISSUES I SHOULD KNOW REGARDING DOUBLE DEPOSITING AND EARLY APPLICATIONS?

> **Myth:** Not adhering to university policies concerning early decision and double depositing is okay.

Truth: In this increasingly complicated admissions world, more and more students are applying early to colleges. At this time, the two early program policies are early action (EA) and early decision (ED). Early action plans are typically nonbinding, which means students can receive an early response to their application, typically by mid-December, but they do not have to commit to the college until the regular reply date of May 1. Early decision plans, in contrast, are binding, so should a student apply to an ED school and get accepted as an ED applicant, they must attend that college and withdraw all applications to other schools.

Mary Maier, director of admissions at Haverford College, stated that "early decision is a great option for students who have done a thorough college search process and have emerged from it with a clear first choice, a school that they know they will be happy attending." Essentially, when you apply early decision to a school, you are saying that if they admit you, you will come. [123]

The ethical issue here is that you made a promise to the ED school that you would withdraw everywhere else if they

---

123 *Haverford College.* "Who should apply Early Decision?" October 1, 2018. Video, 1:23.

admitted you. By doing so, they forego admitting someone else who would actually attend that school. Typically, if you are applying to an ED school, you can only submit an application to that school, as it is sometimes prohibited to apply both ED and EA simultaneously. So, you must not be dishonest in the process. The truth is, if the college that admitted you early decision finds out that you did not withdraw the rest of your applications, it could rescind its offer of admission. So, get onto that computer and figure out how to withdraw applications from your other schools so you can be as honest as possible in the process. If you are in need of financial aid to attend college, most people suggest that you do not apply ED to a school, because you will not be able to compare financial aid packages among various schools.

Another ethical issue in the college admissions process is double depositing. Sometimes a student will get into a few schools they are not very excited about and then get waitlisted at their first-choice school. Double depositing is the act of submitting multiple deposits to schools you have been accepted to as a way to signal multiple colleges that you will be attending their school in the fall.[124] Typically, students do this because they are waiting on a response from a school they received a waitlist decision from. Double depositing is not looked upon kindly in the admissions community and may backfire on an applicant.

Bruce J. Poch, VP and dean of admissions at Pomona College, said depositing checks to two colleges is an "utterly selfish thing to do."

---

124 Finder, Alan, "Admissions Officials Lament Practice of Signing On With More Than One College," *The New York Times*, May 20, 2006.

"It's fundamentally dishonest to say to more than one college that that's where you're going to be in the fall," said Dan Rosenfield, dean of enrollment management at the University of Louisiana at Lafayette, "and it's not a victimless crime."[125]

While it is not appropriate to submit multiple deposits to multiple schools, if your dream college placed you on the waitlist, then you can submit a deposit to one school as a backup until your waitlisted school accepts you. But it is not ethical to submit a deposit to two schools while you wait for your first-choice college to respond.

Bottom Line: As the college admissions process becomes more competitive and cutthroat, now more than ever we must refocus on bringing ethics front and center so all students can benefit from a fair system. Students are understandably trying to hedge their bets as they compete for competitive spots, but you must be reading the admissions policies for the schools you are applying to. Some colleges reserve the right to rescind an offer of admission if they discover a student has made a double deposit or broke an early decision agreement. The admissions world is incredibly small and news travels fast, so you need to adhere to fair policies and procedures in the process. Most admissions offices accept calls from 9 a.m. to 5 p.m. Monday through Friday to answer questions from prospective applicants. Take advantage of those opportunities. If you have paid a deposit and need to withdraw, you will have to do so in writing to the office of admissions. Please make sure the student writes

---

125 Ibid.

and signs the letter—not the parent. The letter should state that you are electing to withdraw and provide an explanation for why you are withdrawing. After you send the letter via mail, also send an email to the admissions office using the same email address you have been corresponding with throughout the process.

SECTION 39: HOW IMPORTANT ARE MY MIDYEAR AND FINAL TRANSCRIPTS DURING SENIOR YEAR?

Myth: I do not have to worry about my grades senior year, especially if I have been admitted early to the college of my choice.

Truth: Although high school seniors may believe that once they submit their applications they can finally relax and slack off, students must continue to keep their grades up, because colleges reserve the right to rescind offers of admission, especially for bad grades. All admission offers are conditional on your academic performance for your entire high school career. Thus, admissions officers look at your midyear and final high school transcripts even after you are admitted, and they have the power to rescind your admittance, place you on academic probation, or even alter your financial aid award during your freshman year of college should your grades slip.

Although falling into "senioritis" is easy, you need to find ways to manage it throughout your senior year. Senioritis refers to the decline in motivation and academic performance in high school seniors.[126] Feel free to talk to your guidance counselor at school if you feel a slump in your grades is inevitable. Usually, an admissions officer will call your guidance counselor first to ask them if they know why the grades have slipped. Admissions officers reserve the right to ask admitted students to explain drops in grades and revoke the letter of admission if they are not satisfied with your response regarding the matter. If your guidance counselor knows about a medical issue or family trauma during senior year, they can provide context to your application before a college admissions officer notices and calls them about it.

Midyear reports are typically sent by your guidance counselor in February, and then the end-of-year grades are sent by June or July. Students may not know their admission is going to be revoked until end of July or early August. If you keep your grades up, you can avoid trouble. Should your grades drop, you should send a note to the admissions office immediately and get ahead of the game.

In that letter or email you submit to the admissions office, be sure to include the following things:

1. Your name, application ID number, and any other identification codes the school provided to you

2. A copy of your transcript in the attachment

3. A thorough explanation of why your grades slipped and what you plan to do to make sure you are on top of your work in college

---

126 College Board, "Senioritis," accessed June 5, 2020.

This note should not be longer than two paragraphs or ten to twelve sentences total. Remember to be honest and sincere upfront. When colleges look at your midyear grade report or the final transcript, they expect students to maintain the same level of academic achievement that led to their initial admittance. Consistency is key here. If you were a straight-A student, colleges expect you will continue to be a straight-A student. If you had occasional B and B- grades sprinkled amid As, colleges expect those grades will be consistent senior year. Grades in the C range and below during senior year should be avoided at all costs.

In addition to keeping up your grades, colleges expect you will take the same rigor of courses under the senior year course list you were initially admitted for. They want to make sure the grades you receive match the course rigor throughout the entirety of your senior year. One way to prevent senior-itis is to ensure that you remain involved and focused in school throughout senior year. Although senior year can be a stressful time, remember that the stakes are high, so you must remain consistent.

Bottom Line: While slipping into senioritis can happen all too easily, you need to maintain a consistent academic record if you do not want the college of your dreams to rescind its offer of admission. Remember that the stakes are really high in this competitive admissions process, and the last thing you want to happen is that you are placed on probation during your first year of college and start off on the wrong path. Colleges are pretty understanding and flexible if special circumstances made your grades drop senior year, but you must reach out to them before they reach out to you. If you get ahead of it, you might fare better. As always, keep in touch with your guidance counselor and teachers throughout senior year. They are your advocates in the process should anything go wrong. You would not want to lose a merit- or need-based scholarship for college because you slacked off senior year.

SECTION 40: HOW SHOULD I PUT IN A GAP YEAR REQUEST?

> **Myth:** Selective universities do not support students who want to take gap years between high school and college.

Truth: You can certainly take a gap year between high school and college. In fact, many selective universities fully support that decision. According to the American Gap Association (AGA), a nonprofit that accredits gap year programs, between thirty and forty thousand high school students are taking time off after high school for a semester or more.[127] With more than 35 percent of high school seniors thinking of taking a gap year, taking time off after high school is certainly spiking in popularity. Typically, gap years refer to the time students take off after high school and before starting college to travel, work, volunteer, etc.

Universities recognize the benefits of taking a gap year for academically motivated high school graduates. AGA research found that 90 percent of students who take a structured gap year return to school within a year and are more likely to

---

127 Gillies, Trent. "Filling in the gap year after high school: Making the most of time off." *CNBC.* May 15, 2016.

graduate on time and with a higher GPA.[128] In our increasingly fast-paced and competitive world, studies have found that taking breaks and time to reflect can be beneficial for today's youth. Students in high school face unprecedented pressure to earn top grades, start new clubs and organizations, volunteer after school, and get into a top-tier university by the end of senior year.

Students who take gap year before enrolling "bring more to their college experience and, as a result, derive more from it," stated Greg Buckles, dean of admissions at Middlebury College.[129] He added, "They also hold a disproportionately high number of leadership positions on campus and, on average, perform better academically."

If you are considering taking a gap year, you should still submit your application during your senior year of high school. Once you are admitted to that college, you can request the gap year after submitting your enrollment deposit.

"Applying by the end of your senior year of high school ensures that you will have access to your school's resources and won't be bogged down with applications and standardized testing during a year that may include travel abroad," advised Michele Hernández, former admissions officer at Dartmouth College. According to Hernández, "You'd be surprised how quickly your high school forgets you. It's really hard to go back and

---

128 Ibid.

129 Middlebury College, "Taking a Gap Year."

ask for teacher recommendations and the other materials you might need after a year has passed."[130]

So, if you are thinking of taking a gap year, apply by the end of your senior year while you still have direct access to your guidance counselor and teachers. It is better to apply to college as a senior in high school than during your gap year, because universities are suspicious when you apply as a gap year student while out of high school. They might think you already committed to another school and are violating another school's policy.

Typically, when you receive your acceptance letter, you must indicate your intention to take a gap year for one year (or sometimes two years) on the enrollment reply form. It is also beneficial to email your regional admissions officer and simply state:

I am pleased to receive an acceptance letter from X school. I plan to enroll at X school, and I am requesting to defer my enrollment until the term beginning [month, year].

Then the admissions officer will likely ask you to write back and tell them what you plan on doing during that time. Most universities will grant a deferral for "almost any reason, but generally not for continued schooling at a high school or university other than the one you were admitted to," explained Matt McGann, former admissions officer at MIT. "I should also note that if your gap year plans are not certain by the May

130 Kyle DeNuccio, "A College Application Guide for Gap Year Students," *The New York Times*, April 6, 2017.

enrollment deadline, you can instead select the 'Enrolling' option on the reply form, and then you can request a deferral any time right up until Registration Day in September."[131]

Once you elect to take a gap year, you are bound to that decision, so only request a gap year if you are committed to taking the year off from school. Remember that your offer of admission will remain active during your time abroad, so you will not lose your enrollment during that time. However, gap year students cannot enroll at another college or university as a full-time degree-seeking student during the gap year, and they cannot take college-level classes they hope to gain credit for. Additionally, deferred students may not apply for admission at any other college or university either in the United States or internationally. Be sure to read the rules and regulations before electing to take the gap year.

Bottom Line: Gap years are becoming an increasingly popular option for high school graduates, and colleges are supportive of their admitted students taking time off before starting college. "No one ever regrets having taken a gap year, but plenty of people regret not having taken one," McGann stated.[132] For further reading on gap years, I recommend buying Kristin M. White's book *The Complete Guide to the Gap Year.* Although our modern society pressures young people to rush through adolescence into the real world, taking some time off to reflect and grow can be beneficial when you transition seamlessly into your college years.

---

131 Matt McGann, "On taking a Gap Year," MIT Admissions, April 11, 2011.
132 Ibid.

CHAPTER 9

SECURE THE FUNDING: PART 1

———

SECTION 41: DOES APPLYING FOR FINANCIAL AID HURT MY CHANCES OF ADMISSION?

Myth: Applying for financial aid will negatively affect my admissions decision.

Truth: With the cost of attendance for several universities slated to increase in the next decade, more and more families are understandably worried about whether they will be able to afford sending their children to college. By 2025, the University of Chicago and at least a handful of other selective US colleges, such as Columbia University and Southern Methodist University, are predicted to have a sticker price of $100,000. In reality, most colleges' students pay less than the sticker price. Most selective colleges seek to build a class that is racially and socioeconomically diverse and provide tuition discounts and scholarship dollars to help students afford these cost-prohibitive universities. If you need financial aid to get through college, it is in your best interest to apply for it and then enroll in the school that gives you the most money, especially during your undergraduate studies.

Now, the question about whether applying for financial aid hurts your chances of admission remains. The truth is that it depends on whether the college you are applying to has a need-blind admissions policy. Need-blind admissions mean the college does not take into account a family's ability to pay when making admissions decisions. Admissions officers at need-blind schools do not even know that you are applying for financial aid at all unless you mention it in your college essay or elsewhere on the application. The schools that follow need-blind admissions will admit students based on academic merit, regardless of whether the student can pay. Over 100 US colleges and universities follow need-blind admissions for US students. Examples of need-blind schools include Princeton, Harvard, Georgetown, MIT, and more.

Need-aware colleges, by contrast, factor in a student's family ability to pay for college in their admissions decisions. These schools do not have unlimited budgets and have to be more cost sensitive as to whether they can afford to fund students applying for financial aid. These schools include Smith, Oberlin, Tufts, Colgate, etc.

Note that colleges with need-blind admissions might not meet the full demonstrated financial need for their admitted students. This is important because you might be able to get into your dream university but then you might not be able to afford it. Fewer than half of the colleges with need-blind admissions meet the full demonstrated need for admitted applicants. By contrast, need-aware policies sometimes give students better financial aid packages when they admit students, because they are picky about whom they offer admission to in the first place and only offer admissions packages to financial aid applicants if they can afford to do so. When you visit a college or call the admissions office, be sure to ask if their university's financial aid office meets the full demonstrated need for admitted students.

Typically, if you are applying as an international student, financial need matters more. Stanford Undergraduate Admissions stated that international students' "request for financial aid will be a factor in [their] admission evaluation."[133] This means that a lot of international hopefuls are sometimes denied admission because of their financial need. Moreover, Stanford said that if international applicants choose not to apply for financial aid, they "are not eligible to apply for financial aid at any time during their four years at Stanford."[134]

Also, some need-blind colleges are only need-blind during the normal review process and tend to not be need-blind for waitlisted students. Audrey Smith, dean of enrollment at Smith College, explained that her school's admissions officers "take out of the class and place on the wait list those with high levels of financial need."[135] If you are in a situation where you have high financial need and you are placed on a waitlist for

---

133 *The Stanford Daily*, "Plan for need-blind admissions for international students," March 9, 2018.

134 Ibid.

135 Kim Clark, "Colleges Where Need for Aid Can Hurt Admission Odds," *U.S. News & World Report*, March 23, 2010.

a school, please get in touch with that school's financial aid office for an estimate of what your package would be like should you be admitted.

Bottom Line: Although applying for financial aid might negatively affect an applicant's chance of admission at some schools, you should still submit your financial aid form to all the schools where you will apply. You do not want to be in a situation where you get into your dream college and cannot pay for it or, worse, have to take out private loans with high interest rates. For many jobs, professional degrees are required or preferred, so you may have to pursue a graduate degree depending on your field of study. You need to get as much scholarship money as possible so you can be more flexible after your undergraduate studies.

SECTION 42: DO I QUALIFY FOR A FEE WAIVER OR ENROLLMENT DEPOSIT DEFERRAL?

> **Myth:** If I cannot afford the application fee or pay the enrollment deposit, I will not be able to attend college.

Truth: The cost of applying to college can start to add up, especially if students are applying to eight or more schools. Application fees range from twenty-five to ninety dollars per college, which may feel out of reach for many applicants and their families. While you cannot simply forgo these fees as they are a required part of the application, you may qualify for a fee waiver that either eliminates or greatly reduces the cost of applying. After you are admitted to the college of your choice, you usually must pay an enrollment deposit fee, and the same principle applies: you can contact the school to either eliminate or lower the price of your enrollment deposit.

Here are several insights on how to acquire those fee waivers from colleges, as explained by the College Board:[136]

- **Insight 1**: Every income-eligible student who takes the SAT or SAT Subject Tests with a fee waiver can apply to over two thousand colleges in the College Board network for free. Students typically receive those fee waivers when they get their SAT scores.

- **Insight 2**: If you are eligible for free or reduced lunch at your high school, your guidance counselor may help you submit a fee waiver form with the National Association for College Admission Counseling (NACAC).

- **Insight 3**: Search for the universities that accept application fee waivers. Sometimes you may be able to request the fee waiver directly from the institution. Some schools have a policy in which you can arrange for an application fee waiver if you attend one of their campus visit days. Feel free to call the admissions office to see if it offers this waiver before scheduling your visit.

- **Insight 4**: Applying through the Coalition, Common, or Universal applications may help you easily qualify for fee waivers for multiple schools at once. Each of these

---

136 College Board, "Application fee waiver," NACAC, accessed June 5, 2020.

application platforms has a process in place to get your applications successfully to the schools.

If you are applying as a transfer applicant, know that the process is different for acquiring those fee waivers. Here are the instructions to follow as explained by the College Board:[137]

- **Private colleges**: Each private college does fee waivers differently for transfer applicants. NACAC and College Board fee waivers do not work for transfer students. On the payment page of the Common App or the school's individual application, select "Other Fee Waiver." Then you may submit a letter from your transfer adviser stating that the application fee would cause financial hardship for you and your family. Feel free to communicate with an admissions officer at the college and explain your situation to them as well. They might have resources you do not know about.

- **Public colleges**: Each public college system does fee waivers differently. In some states, like California, students who are low-income can apply for fee waivers directly on their applications. Fill in the family's financial information where requested. Students in community college programs automatically qualify. Other students will most likely qualify if they would have qualified as high school seniors.

After you are admitted, you are expected to pay an enrollment deposit to secure your spot in the class. The deposit fee ranges

---

137 "Fee Waivers for Transfer Students' College Applications," Get Me To College, accessed June 5, 2020.

from $500 to $900. Since you are already admitted and the school wants you, you have some leverage here. Typically, you will still have to pay something, but the amount can be greatly reduced. Call the financial aid office for the school you will attend and negotiate the amount for the enrollment deposit.

Bottom Line: Most two-year colleges are free to apply to, so no fee waiver is needed. For many four-year colleges, you may apply for a fee waiver for application fees at the standardized test examination. You are eligible to receive fee waivers if and only if college application fees would create a financial burden or hardship for you and your family. Note that your immigration status does not matter for most private college fee waivers. Students who were eligible for fee waivers college entrance exams, such as the SAT or ACT, are usually also eligible for college application fee waivers. Do not be afraid to use the fee waivers. You can use as many as you need. Although not every college provides fee waivers, a large amount do provide them. If you have questions, call the admissions office for each school on your list to learn about their policies for application fee and enrollment deposit waivers.

SECTION 43: WHAT ARE THE HIDDEN COSTS OF APPLYING TO COLLEGE THAT I SHOULD BE AWARE OF?

Myth: The only cost associated with applying to college is that of application fees.

Truth: While most applicants know that you have to pay for the application fees for each school you apply to, but did you know that just visiting a college for an information session and campus tour can potentially cost your family upward of $500? Bruce Horovitz from *The Washington Post* once said that "whatever you think you know about college costs, you're wrong. It's going to cost more. Lots more."[138] The truth is that applying to college is going to be expensive, and you need to prepare well in advance for what the overall costs will look like. In addition to application fees for each university you apply to, you will also need to take into account additional fees such as transportation, standardized test preparation, and more. This section of the book will help you budget accordingly so there are no surprises on the back end.

Below are the top ten additional costs you will need to account for when budgeting for the application process:

1. **College visits (estimated cost = $500–$5,000)**: Visiting college campuses is crucial when trying to decide which school is a great fit for the applicant. Remember to take into account the cost of flights, meals, hotel accommodations, ground transportation, and miscellaneous considerations such as buying college apparel from the bookstore. Visiting colleges by the summer before senior year is worth your time.

2. **SAT, ACT, and SAT Subject Test preparation (estimated cost = $250–$10,000)**: Preparing for the SAT, ACT, and/or SAT Subject Tests can cost anywhere from zero dollars though free online tutorials to tens of thousands of dollars through tutoring services. In addition, many students

---

138 Bruce Horovitz, "Colleges hidden costs: What the admissions office doesn't tell you," *The Washington Post*, November 26, 2016.

have to buy the test prep books to prepare for the exams. Some schools require additional testing, i.e., Subject Tests on various topics or TOEFL, for students whose primary language is not English.

3. **Sending entrance exam scores (estimated cost = $50–$500):** The main SAT exam costs fifty dollars, and you are able to send those scores to four schools for free. Each additional score report costs the applicant eleven dollars per school. For SAT Subject Tests, sending scores costs thirty-five dollars for nonlanguage tests and forty-six for language tests. The ACT costs thirty-five dollars per exam and comes with four free score reports. Each additional report costs eleven dollars each. The ACT plus Writing exam, which is required by some colleges, costs fifty dollars.

4. **Nonrefundable application fees (estimated cost = $250–$750):** Most students are applying to between eight to ten schools. Application fees range from twenty-five to ninety dollars per school, with an average price tag of forty dollars, as per *U.S. News & World Report*. College application fees can add up really quickly. If you have financial difficulties, be sure to ask for a fee waiver.

5. **Financial aid application fees (estimated cost = $0–$25):** More than 1.4 million high school graduates did not bother to fill out the FAFSA last year. This group of students would have qualified for about $2.7 billion in federal financial aid, which amounts to almost $2,000 per student. The FAFSA is free to apply for, and some schools require you to also fill out the CSS Profile, which costs

about twenty-five dollars. Fill out the forms, as you do not want to leave money on the table.

6. **High school transcripts (estimated cost = $10–$150):** Some high schools send transcripts free of charge to universities, while many are beginning to charge to send transcripts to each college.

7. **Registration with the NCAA for student athletes (estimated cost = $90–$150):** If you intend to play a sport in college, you must pay to register with NCAA. The fee for certification accounts with the NCAA costs $90 for US and Canadian athletes and $150 for international athletes.

8. **Application guidance via college consultants (estimated cost = $1,000–$25,000):** Some students and their families choose to hire college admissions consultants for guidance during the application process. These consultants typically provide guidance with college essays, building the college list, and more. Disclaimer: Some scams may be associated with hiring college consultants. Beware of those who claim they can guarantee admissions for a fee.

9. **Accepted student weekend trips (estimated cost = $500–$2,000):** After you receive your offers from schools, you may have difficulty making the decision to enroll without visiting during the open house for admitted students. The cost for these trips may include overnight stays at hotels and travel costs. Usually, meals are provided by the host university. Some free diversity fly-in programs exist for low-income students.

10. **Nonrefundable tuition and housing deposit (estimated cost = $50–$900):** Every university requires a deposit that confirms enrollment for a student in college. Some schools require you to submit an additional housing deposit to secure your spot in student housing on or near campus.

Bottom Line: Applying to college is getting increasingly more expensive. All the costs listed above are expenses you must pay before you are even accepted to a college. As students apply to more schools, the fees associated with making sure that your application is competitive and complete can truly add up. You need to create a budget based on estimated costs associated with the college application process so you do not encounter surprises. Of course, there are always ways to find financial assistance from the schools you apply to. Should you have difficulty paying for something, the best route is to call the admissions office of the universities on your list and ask for assistance. You should not be ashamed to do so, as many colleges allocate these funds for the purpose of helping students seamlessly apply to their schools, which will increase the socioeconomic diversity of the student body.

SECTION 44: HOW CAN I QUALIFY FOR IN-STATE VERSUS OUT-OF-STATE TUITION BENEFITS?

Myth: Qualifying for in-state tuition anywhere but in your home state is impossible.

Truth: As you are looking at colleges, you are probably noticing that out-of-state tuition is typically higher than in-state tuition. This difference in the cost of attendance varies by state. Kerry Traylor, founder of College Strategy Experts, said that for a lot of students, "public universities are going to be the cheapest schools for them because states are going to give substantial discounts to students who reside within their state."[139] For example, at North Carolina State University, the in-state tuition costs $8,880 and the out-of-state tuition costs $26,399. That's almost three times more! You may want to attend college in a different state than your hometown— but you may be wondering how you can benefit from that opportunity to get in-state tuition at an out-of-state school.

In-state tuition rules are designed to weed out nonresidents. However, that doesn't mean you cannot proudly attend school in another state at a discounted price.

Take, for example, the story of Allie Hanson, a nineteen-year old from New York, published by *U.S. News & World Report*. Because she "got a 30 on the ACT, they waived out-of-state tuition and gave her half off in state tuition" to attend Mississippi State. So instead of paying the $20,900 out-of-state sticker price to attend Mississippi State University, Hanson will only pay about $4,000 in tuition.[140]

"Most flagship state schools are not going to give a lot of money to your average or even above average out-of-state student unless you're the cream of the crop," said Sarah Langford,

---

139 College Admissions, "Cost of in-state vs out-of-state tuition," February 8, 2016, video, 1:36.

140 Farran Powell, "3 Facts About Aid, Tuition for Out-of-State Students," *U.S. News & World Report*, October 24, 2016.

founder of a college advising firm. "So, if you are thinking about college affordability and an out of state public school, it is time to hit the books!"[141]

"Some institutions have historically offered in-state tuition to residents in bordering counties of a neighboring state," said David L. Wright, a senior research analyst at the nonprofit State Higher Education Executive Office. "Then there are reciprocity programs, which offer reduced tuition to nearby state residents."[142]

In some states these programs do not exist, so exceptions to residency rules likely do apply for these groups:

1. Children of active-duty military service members are a notable exception, with policies varying by state.

2. Children of divorced parents (i.e., who is paying for school).

3. Children of state-college alumni.

4. Students with athletic, musical, or other desired talents, as well.

5. Students who sign a pledge to work and stay in that area after college.

6. Academic achievement based on standardized test scores.

---

141 Ibid.

142 Melissa Ezarik, "Busted: Six top myths of in-state tuition eligibility," Bankrate, August 15, 2005.

If for some reason you are not approved for in-state tuition at an out-of-state school, it might be "cheaper to attend a private college and university," according to Kerry Taylor. She added that "public schools out of state can actually be the most expensive schools for students, because number one, you're paying out-of-state prices. Number two, public schools are the schools often that are going to meet a lesser percentage of your demonstrated financial need. And number three, often public schools are the schools that are going to give more of their money away in the form of loans that you have to pay back in interest, instead of money in the form of grants and scholarships, which you don't have to pay back."[143]

There are pros and cons to attending in-state versus out-of-state schools that applicants should be aware of. If you choose to stay in state, you will be attending a university that the majority of your friends may also be attending, which could make for an easier transition. If you tend to get homesick or have a sick relative at home you need to be there for, staying local might be even more cost and time effective.

But if you are looking for a fresh start and want some independence, picking a school out of state may be wise. You will be able to interact with folks you have never met before, which might help you grow in your confidence. College is a time to explore who you are and pursue your passions. You should visit many colleges both in-state and out of state before making a firm decision on where you want to spend the next four years of your life.

---

143 College Admissions, "Cost of in-state vs out-of-state tuition," February 8, 2016, video, 1:36.

Bottom Line: You can qualify for in-state tuition for an out-of-state school, but you must do your research ahead of time. The key is checking on financial implications and policies while you build your college list. Be sure to visit the financial aid office of the schools you are applying to and ask the college for residency standards by state. By speaking directly to a financial aid representative, you can develop a plan or approach that can make attending college affordable for you during your four undergraduate years.

SECTION 45: IS THERE A WAY TO APPEAL FINANCIAL AID AWARDS?

Myth: I cannot negotiate my financial aid package.

Truth: The overall price of attending college these days has increased astronomically. With such large costs, one of the looming questions on every applicant's mind is *How can I afford to attend college?* In addition to working on college application files, students need to simultaneously apply for financial aid to procure scholarships that lessen the cost of attending college and reduce student debt. Financial aid is separated into two forms: need-based and merit-based financial aid. Need-based financial aid is given solely based on your family's income and assets, whereas merit-based financial aid is given purely for academic ability.

You will also need to complete two forms: the FAFSA and CSS Profile. These forms are created by the US Department of Education to qualify you and your family for financial aid.

After you have completed all the forms necessary (i.e., FAFSA and CSS) and you are offered admission, your admission letter usually comes with a financial aid award. If you receive the financial aid package and realize you did not receive enough scholarship money, or the parent and student contribution expectation is out of reach for your family, you should call the school's financial aid office and appeal the award. Although not all financial aid appeals are successful, doing so is worth a try. If you write a good financial aid appeal letter that hits on several key points, you will have a shot at receiving more financial aid.

Students and their families are not always aware you can appeal your financial aid award decision. "Too often families think of the financial aid award letter as being set in stone and not subject to appeal," said Mark Kantrowitz, publisher and vice president of research for Savingforcollege.com. "The first sign there might be an issue is if the financial aid offer is not merely a harsh assessment of your ability to pay, but an impossible assessment. Chances are there is some bit of information the financial aid office was unaware of when they calculated your financial aid package."[144]

The first thing you need to do when contacting the financial aid office is to figure out who your direct contact is within that office. Some schools assign financial aid officers by applicant's last name and others classify it by your location or region. If you cannot find the information online, feel free to call the financial aid office and ask them for your financial

---

144 Mark Kantrowitz, "How to Appeal for More Financial Aid for College," *Saving for College*, January 21, 2019.

aid representative's name, direct phone number, and email address. Remember that since you have already been admitted, you have a ton of leverage.

After you have called your financial aid representative to discuss the process of appealing financial aid, write and send a physical letter. Be sure to discuss any circumstances that may have changed in the past year that the financial aid office did not know about or consider in their decision process. Be as specific as possible.

According to Saving for College, some examples of these special circumstances include:[145]

1. Job loss or decrease in income

2. Divorce or separation of a dependent student's parents

3. Death of a dependent student's parent

4. Special-needs or disabled children

5. Unreimbursed medical and dental expenses

6. Catastrophic loss, such as damage or loss from a natural disaster

7. Textbook costs beyond the standard allowance in the cost of attendance

---

145 Ibid.

8. Change in the student's marital status

9. Dependency override

10. End of child support, Social Security benefits for a child, or alimony payments

You'll have to submit all of the documentation necessary for success, including copies of layoff notices, medical/dental bills, bank of brokerage account statements, or letters from people who are unrelated to the family, teachers, social workers, doctors, etc. You may also submit letters from priests, rabbis, pastors, and other clergy members. The documentation must be related to the special circumstances listed above.

A sample financial aid appeal letter should be concise and should discuss the special circumstances that have affected your family's ability to pay the suggested amount. It should include something along the lines of this:

Template for Financial Aid Appeal Letter

[Mr./Ms.] [Last name]:

*I am delighted to know that I have been
accepted to [X university]. I have reviewed
my financial aid award for this school year.
While I appreciate the financial assistance
that I received as per the financial award, I am
reaching out to you to request reconsideration
due to a significant change in my family's
circumstances. The circumstances that have*

changed thus far include [X]. As a result, I
would like to appeal my financial aid package
for a larger one to further my education.

I have attached documents with a detailed
explanation of the reasons why I need additional
financial assistance. Please let me know if any
additional information is required. When is
the best time to speak with you via phone or in
person? You may reach me at [phone number]
or [insert email address]. Your consideration
is appreciated.

Best,
[X]

Be sure to attach documents with your appeal letter. Since most universities will not return files you send them, you should send copies of your documents and keep the original letter. It is suggested that you mail the appeal letter and documents to the financial aid office through certified mail and then also email the appeal letter, so it automatically gets uploaded to the folder.

Bottom Line: Colleges want the students they admit making a deposit and enrolling in their university. They do not want to lose quality students for financial reasons. Elite universities have donors who give them restricted funds they must use through scholarships every year and they must give the money out solely for the purpose of scholarships. Do not miss out on your piece of the pie. Be sure to fill out the FAFSA and CSS Profile as soon as possible to ensure that you, at the very least, receive a financial aid package. If that package is not enough, be sure to appeal. Remember to be polite in the process of appealing for financial aid. Thank the college financial aid administrator for taking the time to consider your appeal. Remember that financial aid offices are busy dealing with many requests, so wait at least three to five days for a response for your appeal. Remember to include your updated contact information in case the financial aid office has any questions for you. If you have not heard back from your financial aid administrator after a week, reach out to them. The more prepared you are to handle the process, the better your chances will be to see some results.

CHAPTER 10

SECURE THE FUNDING: PART 2

SECTION 46: WILL ROTC PROVIDE ME WITH A FULL SCHOLARSHIP?

Myth: If I enroll in ROTC (Reserve Officers' Training Corps), I will automatically receive a full scholarship to college.

Truth: While it is a great program, enrolling in ROTC does not guarantee you will get a full scholarship. "We do have scholarships that we offer out and those cover tuition and fees and some other things, but that is not a guarantee," said Travis Wright, enrollment and recruiting officer for Army ROTC at the University of Massachusetts Amherst. "It's a competitive process just like receiving any other scholarship."[146]

---

146 Deborah Ziff Soriano, "3 Myths About Army ROTC Scholarships for College," *U.S. News & World Report*, March 4, 2020.

ROTC, in and of itself, is simply a chance to study and serve while earning your undergraduate degree. It is first and foremost an opportunity to get leadership training while in college. Should you commit to joining ROTC with a scholarship, you can train in military science and take regular classes with everyone else, with the intention to enlist as an officer in the US Army, Navy, or Air Force when you graduate. ROTC scholarships are awarded in two different ways: students can compete nationally for a scholarship during their senior year of high school, or they can join ROTC once they get to college and compete for a scholarship at the campus level.

You have to meet certain requirements to be part of the ROTC program. You must:

- Be a US citizen.

- Be between the ages of seventeen and twenty-six.

- Have a high school GPA of at least 2.50.

- Have a high school diploma or equivalent.

- Score a minimum of 1000 on the SAT (math/verbal) or 19 on the ACT (excluding the required writing test scores).

- Meet physical fitness standards.

- Agree to accept a commission and serve in the Army on active duty or in a reserve component (Army Reserve or Army National Guard).[147]

Typically, students participate in Junior ROTC (JROTC) while in high school to gain training as good citizens, and they use JROTC as a vehicle to earn an ROTC scholarship. While JROTC experience is not a prerequisite to participate in ROTC and earn the ROTC scholarship, it does help high school students develop excellent leadership skills.

According to Senior Navy Science Officer James Boyer, students who have participated in JROTC programs "have a fairly good background to carry into ROTC service, adding students know the history, chain of command and general expectations."[148]

At the national level, "about twelve thousand high school seniors compete for about two thousand Army ROTC scholarships. About half of those are three-year scholarships, and the other half are four-year scholarships," said Tony Wolf, recruiting operations officer for the University of Iowa Army ROTC program. "Do well in school. Prepare yourself for the ACT. Ask to belong to the National Honor Society," Wolf continued. "When you look at a kid out there being active, they're naturally a great candidate for the Army ROTC and the possibility of a full-tuition scholarship."[149]

---

147 Ibid.

148 US Army, "Army ROTC," accessed June 5, 2020.

149 Deborah Ziff Soriano, "3 Myths About Army ROTC Scholarships for College."

If you are applying for a scholarship, you will need to create a MY GOARMY account. After you have created the account, you will be sent to the login page, where you will use your account information to apply for the scholarship application site. Be sure to allow plenty of time to complete the application and get the necessary recommendation letter from someone who knows your skills and leadership capabilities inside and outside of the classroom.

If you are lucky enough to get the scholarship, you have a few things to consider before accepting the offer. When a student accepts a scholarship, they sign a contract with ROTC promising to hit certain academic benchmarks and to serve in the armed forces after graduation. This is called "contracting," Wright explained.

If you are awarded a scholarship, you must be willing to make certain commitments:

- An eight-year service commitment with the Army.

- Serve full time in the Army for four years and four years with the Individual Ready Reserve (IRR).

- Selected Cadets may choose to serve part time in the Army Reserve or Army National Guard while pursuing a civilian career.[150]

---

150 US Army, "Army ROTC."

Bottom line: ROTC recognition does not guarantee you a full ride to college, but you have a possibility to apply for the scholarship if you meet certain requirements. When you enroll in ROTC, you do not join the Army, but you will receive college credit for the courses you take. In addition, you will build some skills in leadership and management that you may carry with you for the rest of your life. ROTC scholarships are typically merit based, which means they are given to you based on your academic achievement and extracurricular activities, rather than your family's income. Be sure to discuss your options with your guidance counselor while you are in high school, as they typically have experience with other students in the past who have pursued this program.

SECTION 47: WHAT ARE THE MOST COMMON MISTAKES FOUND WHEN FILLING OUT THE FAFSA AND CSS PROFILE?

> **Myth:** I'll never qualify for any financial aid because my family makes too much money.

Truth: Not all financial aid opportunities are need based. Your family may receive merit-based aid or student loans regardless of family income, but the applicant has to apply for financial aid to receive it.

FAFSA stands for the Free Application for Federal Student Aid. Submitting this form qualifies your family for not only need-based financial aid but also federal student loans, state grants, work-study opportunities, merit-based scholarships, college programs, and more. The application is free and available online.

Unfortunately, only 77 percent of families submitted the FAFSA form last year, leaving plenty of money on the table, according to the "How America Pays for College" snapshot from higher education lender Sallie Mae and its Ipsos research partner.[151]

Of those who don't file the FAFSA, "39 percent didn't think they'd qualify, 29 percent didn't file because they didn't know about it or missed the deadline, and 27 percent were missing information, didn't have time or felt the process was too complicated," according to Sallie Mae.[152]

Those assumptions are by far the biggest mistakes that eligible families are making. You have to apply for financial aid to receive something. Make sure you apply even if you think you will not qualify. Many parents wrongly assume they will not get any money at all. The fact is that schools, particularly competitive ones, are very freely discounting the sticker price. Middle-class families making six-figure incomes may be eligible for $10,000, $15,000, or $20,000 a year in need-based grants. The amount you get really depends on several factors, such as gross income, number of children in college, and assets.

The second biggest mistake is putting incorrect information on the forms. Putting wrong information in there is very easy. All

---

151 Steve Rosen, "Not enough parents realize the importance of FAFSA. Here's what families of college kids should know," *Chicago Tribune*, August 22, 2019.

152 Ibid.

the numbers must add up. Do not mix up assets. Money held in a child's name can count against you a lot more than money held in the parents' name. Also, be sure to only add the assets they are asking for. Part of this mistake is including assets that do not need to be included. The form clearly says you do not include the value of your primary home. So, in terms of assets, the home you live in is not counted, nor is retirement, so they are not going to look at either of those things when designing the financial aid package.

The third biggest mistake is not following up with the schools after you submit the financial aid forms. After you submit the forms, you are not done. You need to make sure they received your forms and to see if they need any other information from you. This is extremely important, as many schools may claim they did not receive the FAFSA. Be sure to get confirmation in writing.

You do not have to wait for tax season to submit the FAFSA. You can use your family's prior-prior year tax information to complete the application for aid. The early bird gets the worm, as the saying goes.

You probably already know about the FAFSA, but around three hundred private colleges require students to submit the CSS Profile in addition to the FAFSA to be considered for school-based scholarships. It costs twenty-five dollars to submit the financial aid form, plus sixteen dollars for each copy if you need to send it to more than one school.

"Many schools are sticklers about it," said Bianca Martinez, a former college adviser with the nonprofit College Advising

Corps, who now consults with students and families privately. "If you don't submit it on time, they deny you institutional funding."[153]

The last secret for accessing more financial aid is that you can actually appeal your award letter that the college gives you—not a lot of people know this. Let us say you get the financial aid award letter back from the college, and it's just not enough money to help pay for your needs: you can actually write a letter to the financial aid office appealing your financial aid award.

Bottom Line: On October 1, the FAFSA and CSS Profile applications open so you can begin filling them out as soon as possible, but not later than February 1. By filling out those two forms, you may become eligible for need-based and merit-based scholarships from the colleges you are accepted to. You never know how much you can qualify for unless you apply. The cost of college education is becoming more out of reach for the average American. Colleges are realizing this fact and are ready to negotiate the terms of payment to get you to commit to them.

SECTION 48: WHAT ARE THE FINANCIAL AID OPTIONS AVAILABLE FOR STUDENTS IN FOSTER CARE?

Myth: I will not be able to afford college as a youth in foster care.

---

153 Teddy Nykiel, "Applying for Financial Aid for College: 6 Tips from Counselors," Nerd Wallet, March 18, 2019.

Truth: Although students in foster care who want to pursue a college degree face significant challenges, certain resources are available to help students enroll in a college program and get the necessary funds to pay for it. At this current moment, "just 50 percent of foster youth graduate from high school, and half of those youth aged out of the system end up either homeless or in prison."[154] These statistics will lead you to believe that foster youth have no chance of pursuing a college degree. But the truth is that help is available, and if these applicants have the desire to pursue a college education, with some research and support, that dream can come true.

Depending on the college that students in foster care choose to attend, they may qualify for institutional scholarships created specifically for their needs, considering their unique challenges. They need to apply for the FAFSA and look at instructions specific to students in the foster youth system. Students in foster care or even formerly in the foster care system are eligible to receive independent student status that will allow the applicant to omit custodial parents' financial information. They need to check off the "Ward/dependency of the state or courts" box on the FAFSA form to receive all grants they are eligible for.[155]

Some schools offering programs include Cleveland State, through the Sullivan-Deckard and Helen Packer Scholarship Opportunity Programs for students who have aged out of the foster care system. Western Michigan University offers the

---

154 Kesha Rashed, "From Foster Care to College," Affordable College Online, accessed May 8, 2020.

155 Ibid.

Seita Scholars Program for foster youth, which provides up to $13,400 per year in scholarship money.

Jennifer Pokempner, director of child welfare policy at Juvenile Law Center, a legal advocacy group in Philadelphia, said the Seita program is "seen as a model." Ensuring that "youth in the child welfare system are positioned to have the same choices that youth outside of the system" have is critically important, she said, and programs like Seita help level the playing field. In West Virginia and Pennsylvania, foster youth are provided with full tuition waivers if they are admitted to a university in that state.[156]

There is also an educational voucher called the ETV (Educational and Training Voucher) Program, which was created by the federal government to support foster youth in their pursuit of postsecondary education with a grant of up to $5,000 per year for eligible students for up to five years of study.[157]

As a current foster youth over age eighteen, you might be eligible to receive extended foster care maintenance payments from your agency that may be provided to you directly in some instances for your room and board. It is important to note that foster care payments you receive should not be reported on the FAFSA as part of your income.

No child should be left behind, no matter their circumstances. Earning a college degree can level the playing field

---

156 Ibid.
157 Ibid.

for foster youth, and it is an important step toward the middle class. By 2020, economists predict that nearly two-thirds of jobs will require education beyond high school.

Here are some things to consider when choosing a college:

1. Do you prefer to live in or near your current community?

2. Does your school offer work-study opportunities so you can work while you pursue a postsecondary degree?

3. Do you prefer to live on campus or commute to campus?

4. Do you plan to work while you pursue a postsecondary degree?

5. Do you need a flexible class schedule?

6. Do you prefer to attend a large or small postsecondary institution?

7. Do you want to participate in student groups and extra-curricular activities?

8. How do your financial aid options (e.g., federal grants and loans, scholarships) compare to the cost of tuition at postsecondary institutions you are considering?

9. Is there a particular program or major you are interested in studying? If so, do the postsecondary institutions you are considering offer this program or major?

10. If you are interested in a particular career, do the postsecondary institutions you are considering offer programs and degrees that meet the educational requirements for that career?

Bottom Line: If you are currently in foster care, remember that a college degree is attainable and affordable. Cordelia Cranshaw, the 2019 Miss District of Columbia USA, stated that arriving at college crystallized the advantages of stability. "For the first time in my life, I did not have to worry about things that were a perpetual distraction from academics, things that no child should be preoccupied with. I had a meal plan, I had housing; I was taking full advantage of the resources available to support my journey out of the foster-care system."[158] Many federal, state, and local resources are available for you to pursue your dream of a college education. Although the obstacles may seem daunting, know that it can be done, and you have some amazing role models from those who have done it before you.

SECTION 49: WHAT ARE THE FINANCIAL AID OPTIONS AVAILABLE FOR INTERNATIONAL STUDENTS?

Myth: Not many options for college funding exist for foreign national students.

Truth: Plenty of scholarship programs fund foreign national (international) students, if you know where to look. You may

---

158 Cordelia Cranshaw, "Student Voice: The long road out of foster care included beauty pageants—and lots of studying," *The Hechinger Report*, July 1, 2019.

be surprised to learn about opportunities for scholarships. But, since resources are limited, you must start the process earlier as an international student. You must begin by reaching out to the college or university you are interested in and ask questions about what type of financial aid opportunities are available. Although most of the scholarship opportunities are merit based for international students, some schools have institutional need-based aid available for international students, but it depends, so you must ask.

You should create a list consisting of schools that are need blind and provide financial aid for international students. Do not be afraid to pick up the phone and call schools, because they typically can provide you with information that is not published on the website. Eric Furda, dean of admissions at the University of Pennsylvania, said that "once admitted to Penn, all students, regardless of country of citizenship, receive a financial aid package that in most cases includes some job on campus, and the rest of the package is institutional grant money, which does not get paid back. No loans are part of the financial aid package and that includes international students."[159]

Evelyn Levinson, international admissions director at American University, pointed out that international students can work up to twenty hours a week on campus with permission from immigration. She added, "You have got to have really good time-management skills, and it's good pocket money;

---

159 Unigo, "What Financial Aid Is Available for International Students?" *U.S. News & World Report*, January 4, 2012.

it will not finance your education, but it will help to defray some costs associated with living on campus."[160]

Some organizations set aside money just for international students who wish to study in the United States.

Note that you must apply to these programs simultaneously to applying to college. You should keep an organized spreadsheet detailing the deadline for every program.

When applying for these scholarships, you need to present a good scholarship essay that will set you apart from the pack. You should get your American friends and advisers to proofread your essays before submitting them to colleges. In addition to preparing essays, you should take the SAT/ACT or TOEFL exam early. Scholarship programs want to see your scores on these exams by the deadline.

Here are some of the many financial aid alternatives available to international students:[161]

- **School loans**: Loans must be repaid to the university, typically with interest.

- **Private loans**: Some private lenders offer loans to international students. Those typically must be repaid with higher interest rates than a school loan.

---

160 GPA Interactive, "Can an International Student get a Job While in the U.S.?" December 9, 2014, video, 2:37.

161 Mohsen Alzahrani, "U.S. Financial Aid Options for International Students," World Education Services, January 16, 2019.

- **The International Education Financial Aid (IEFA) organization**: IEFA has partnered with the leading provider of international student loan programs to provide students around the world with financial aid options to fund their education abroad.

- **Scholarships and grants provided by the university**: Each university has its own scholarships and grants. Students can contact the admissions officer or financial aid officer at their school to learn about these scholarships and how to apply for them. (Scholarships and grants are not paid back.)

- **Scholarships and grants offered by departments within the university**: Some university professors partner with organizations and centers to conduct research. These funds can be used by professors to recruit research team members. Students can contact their department and advisers to learn about these scholarships and grants, and whether they extend to international students as well.

Bottom Line: Although the hardest part for international students applying to US colleges is the question of funding, you can find many options for financial aid if you are willing to prepare in advance. Although the resources tend to be limited, financial funding is available to support your goals. Do not be discouraged. US universities have institutional priorities to increase geographic diversity on their college campuses. For additional funding opportunities, you should contact the officials at the US embassy in your home country for additional advice and support.

SECTION 50: HOW CAN I USE THE NET PRICE CALCULATOR TO PREDICT MY FINANCIAL AWARD PACKAGE?

> **Myth:** The net price calculator gives me a guarantee of what my financial aid package will look like.

Truth: The net price calculator gives applicants an estimate of how much you and your family will contribute to college fees. It is not a guarantee of how much money you will receive in scholarships, but it certainly does give you an idea of how much need-based and/or merit-based aid you could potentially receive and how much you will potentially have to contribute to that university should you be admitted. Although colleges are becoming more and more expensive, students are paying less than the sticker price to attend college because of financial aid.

What is the net price?

According to the College Board, the net price is the sticker price for a college, including tuition, room/board, and student fees minus the scholarships (need and merit based) and education tax benefits you have the potential to receive.[162] The net price is what you pay to the college. It is specific to you based on your personal financial circumstances and the college's financial aid rules and regulations.

---

162 CollegeBoard, "The College Board's Net Price Calculator," Accessed May 8, 2020.

Every college has its own net price calculator, and the school's financial aid office calculates your demonstrated need. But you can also use its net price calculator online before applying for financial aid to get an estimate of what the school may provide you. The only guaranteed price is the one the school calculates. The methodology and tools used by the different colleges to determine what your family can contribute to college costs vary per school. You must enter consistent data on all the calculators so your comparisons between schools will be more valid.

Chris Cooper, VP and dean of admissions and financial aid of Davidson College, warns family to "not assume that the cost found from using the net price calculator at one liberal arts college will be the same at all other colleges." Admissions Officer Amin Gonzalez from Yale University added that it is "important to understand that the information that you put in is going to result in a return sort of a prediction, but not a guaranteed offer, financially, so it's to your benefit to use as current information as you have."[163]

Here is the information you will need to fill out the net price calculator:

- **Primary family residence**: number of people in your family and number of children in college.

- **Income information**: parent income/gross wages, interest/dividend income, business/farm income, and real estate income.

---

163 *Davidson College*, "Using the Net Price Calculator," October 4, 2011, video, 2:29.

- **Asset information**: parent assets in cash and investments, real estate equity (not home equity), and student assets.

After you fill out the form, you will either get need-based scholarship, merit-based scholarship, or a combination of both. Getting one form of aid is not easier than the other; which you get simply depends on which requirements you meet and which form of aid is available at the college you apply to. Merit-based aid does not take into account an applicant's family's ability to pay for school when making the financial aid decision. It is based solely on academic achievement and leadership experience. Some colleges that offer large merit-based scholarships include Duke University, the George Washington University, Wesleyan University, Swarthmore College, and Bard College.

Nowadays, more selective schools are shying away from merit-based scholarship and offering more need-based aid instead.

Need-based aid is offered to students based on their family's income. Need-based aid does not mean no loans. Some colleges, such as Harvard University and Princeton University, have a no-loan need-based policy for undergraduate students. But most universities offer need-based financial aid that consists of a combination of grants (which you do not have to pay back), student loans (subsidized and unsubsidized), and work-study options.

Here are some key terms to learn before evaluating your financial aid award, as described by the federal student aid website:

- **Grants**: Grants and scholarships are typically free grant money—financial aid that does not have to be repaid. Grants are often need-based aid, while scholarships are usually merit-based aid.

- **Federal Pell Grants**: Usually awarded only to undergraduate students who display exceptional financial need and have not earned a bachelor's, graduate, or professional degree. A Federal Pell Grant, unlike a loan, does not have to be repaid, except under certain circumstances.

- **Direct subsidized loans:** Loans made to eligible undergraduate students who demonstrate financial need to help cover the costs of higher education at a college or career school.

- **Direct unsubsidized loans:** Loans made to eligible undergraduate, graduate, and professional students, but eligibility not based on financial need.

- **Federal work-study**: Provides part-time jobs for undergraduate and graduate students with financial need, allowing them to earn money to help pay education expenses.

Bottom line: The net price calculator provides an estimate of how much you will contribute to college fees, but it is not a guarantee. Using the net price calculator to estimate the cost of college is important. But, in order to receive both merit- and need-based financial aid, you must submit the FAFSA and CSS Profile by February 1. According to the US Department of Education, net price is "the amount that a student pays to attend an institution in a single academic year AFTER subtracting scholarships and grants the student receives." Using the net price calculators can be exhausting and time consuming, but they are worth using as you build your college list.

CONCLUSION

You have made it to the end! Congratulations.

No matter the hardship and no matter the stakes, your dreams of pursuing higher education are valid. If you want to go to college, do not let anyone stop you from achieving that goal. I am certain that if you use this book as a resource, you will be one step closer to achieving your dreams. The college application process not only prepares you to reflect on your life but also allows you to think about who you were and who you are becoming. As you write your college essays and request letters of recommendation from your teachers, you become more confident in getting things done. The tools you develop will help you as you seek to embark on your careers later on, because once you go through this process, you are forever changed.

When I started my publishing journey, I did not know how much positive feedback I would get from high school students. They tell me how happy they are that I made this information available to them. This experience has been cathartic for me as a college graduate and former admissions officer to give you behind-the-scenes information that is up to date in this increasingly competitive college application environment.

My hope is that, if this book has helped you in any way, you will consider writing a review. Reviews are important to spread the word and message to a wider audience. They are one of the most powerful things you can do to help this book reach other students in need of guidance. I read every single message and piece of feedback I receive and share that information with others who may find this book useful.

Like the African proverb says, if you want to go quickly, go alone. If you want to go further, go together. Let's invite others to learn how to succeed in the college application and financial aid process.

ACKNOWLEDGMENTS

————

I would like to express my deepest gratitude to everyone who helped me publish this book. It took a village to get this book out to the world, and I am grateful for a number of mentors and colleagues who encouraged me to start this work as it will have a far-reaching impact for those trying to navigate the college admissions process.

At Georgetown University, I thank Professor Eric Koester and Brian Bies, of New Degree Press, for providing me the platform, team, and weekly guidance from start to finish. I would like to thank my editors: Stephanie McKibben, Jonathan Jordan, Jamie T., Amanda Brown, etc. I would also like to thank my colleagues on the admissions staff at Georgetown University for their support during my time working in admissions.

GLOSSARY

———

What's the difference between early action and early decision policies? What's a secondary school record? When you are applying to college, you may come across many unfamiliar terms. This glossary will help you understand and make sense of the information you absorb as you go through the college application process.

These definitions are derived from many sources. Primarily, I used the Common Data Set's definitions. The Common Data Set (CDS) initiative is a collaborative effort among data providers in the higher education community and publishers as represented by the College Board, Peterson's, and *U.S. News & World Report*. The combined goal of this collaboration is to improve the quality and accuracy of information provided to all involved in a student's transition into higher education, as well as to reduce the reporting burden on data providers. Additional definitions are pulled from the College Board.

ADMISSIONS DEFINITIONS:

ACT: A standardized college admission test. It features four main sections: English, math, reading, and science—as well as an optional essay section.

Admitted student: Applicant who is offered admission to a degree-granting program at an educational institution.

Application fee: The amount of money an institution charges for processing a student's application for acceptance. This amount is not creditable toward tuition and required fees, nor is it refundable if the student is not admitted to the institution.

Articulation agreement: An agreement between two-year and four-year colleges that makes it easier to transfer credits between them. It spells out which courses count for degree credit and what grades you need to earn to get credit.

Candidates Reply Date Agreement (CRDA): An agreement many colleges follow that gives applicants until May 1 to accept or decline offers of admission. This agreement gives students time to get responses from most of the colleges they have applied to before deciding on one.

Class rank: The relative numerical position of a student in their graduating class, calculated by the high school on the basis of grade-point average, whether weighted or unweighted.

Coalition Application: A standard application form accepted by members of the Coalition for Access, Affordability, and Success. You can use this application to apply to any of the more than ninety colleges and universities that are members of the coalition.

College application essay: An essay that a college requires students to write and submit as part of their application. Some colleges offer applicants specific questions to answer, while others simply ask applicants to write about themselves. Colleges may refer to this as a "personal statement." Learn more about college application essays on the College Board's website.

College preparatory program: Courses in academic subjects (English, history and social studies, foreign languages, mathematics, science, and the arts) that stress preparation for college or university study.

Common Application: The standard application form distributed by the National Association of Secondary School Principals for a large number of private colleges who are members of the Common Application Group.

Cross-registration: A system whereby students enrolled at one institution may take courses at another institution without having to apply to the second institution.

Deferred admission: The practice of permitting admitted students to postpone enrollment, usually for a period of one academic term or one year.

Double major: Program in which students may complete two undergraduate programs of study simultaneously.

Dual enrollment: A program through which high school students may enroll in college courses while still enrolled in high school. Students are not required to apply for admission to the college in order to participate.

Early action: An admission plan that allows students to apply and be notified of an admission decision well in advance of the regular notification dates. If admitted, the candidate is not committed to enroll; the student may reply to the offer under the college's regular reply policy.

Early admission: A policy under which students who have not completed high school are admitted to and enroll full time in college, usually after completion of their junior year.

Early decision: A plan that permits students to apply and be notified of an admission decision (and financial aid offer if applicable) well in advance of the regular notification date. Applicants agree to accept an offer of admission and, if admitted, to withdraw their applications from other colleges. Early-decision applicants have three possible decisions: admitted, denied, or not admitted but forwarded for consideration with the regular applicant pool, without prejudice.

Extracurricular activities (as admission factor): Special consideration in the admissions process given for participation in both school and non-school-related activities of interest to the college, such as clubs, hobbies, student government, athletics, and performing arts.

First-time, first-year (freshman) student: A student attending any institution for the first time at the undergraduate level.

Includes students enrolled in the fall term who attended college for the first time in the prior summer term. Also includes students who entered with advanced standing (college credits earned before graduation from high school).

Geographical residence (as admission factor): Special consideration in the admissions process given to students from a particular region, state, or country of residence.

Grade-point average (academic high school GPA): The sum of grade points a student has earned in secondary school divided by the number of courses taken. The most common system of assigning numbers to grades counts four points for an A, three points for a B, two points for a C, one point for a D, and no points for an E or F. Unweighted GPAs assign the same weight to each course. Weighting gives students additional points for their grades in advanced or honors courses.

Need-blind admission: A policy of making admissions decisions without considering the financial circumstances of applicants. Colleges that use this policy may not offer enough financial aid to meet a student's full need.

Priority date or deadline: The date by which your application—whether for college admission, student housing, or financial aid—must be received to be given the strongest consideration.

Public institution: An educational institution whose programs and activities are operated by publicly elected or appointed school officials, and which is supported primarily by public funds.

Rolling admission: An admission policy of considering each application as soon as all required information (such as high school records and test scores) has been received, rather than setting an application deadline and reviewing applications in a batch. Colleges that use a rolling admission policy usually notify applicants of admission decisions quickly.

SAT: The College Board's standardized college admission test. Learn more about the exam on the College Board's website.

SAT Subject Tests: Hourlong, content-based college admission tests that allow you to showcase achievement in specific subject areas: English, history, math, science, and languages. Some colleges use Subject Tests to place students into the appropriate courses as well as to make admissions decisions.

Secondary school record (as admission factor): Information maintained by the secondary school that may include such elements as the student's high school transcript, class rank, GPA, and teacher and counselor recommendations.

Talent/ability (as admission factor): Special consideration given to students with demonstrated talent/abilities in areas of interest to the institution (e.g., sports, the arts, languages, etc.).

Transcript: The official record of your coursework at a school or college. Your high school transcript is usually required for college admission and for some financial aid packages.

Transfer applicant: An individual who has fulfilled the institution's requirements to be considered for admission (including payment or waiving of the application fee, if any) and who has previously attended another college or university and earned college-level credit.

Tuition: Amount of money charged to students for instructional services. Tuition may be charged per term, per course, or per credit.

Undergraduate: A student enrolled in a four- or five-year bachelor's degree program, an associate degree program, or a vocational or technical program below the baccalaureate.

Universal College Application: A standard application form accepted by all colleges that are Universal College Application members. You can fill out this application once and submit it to anyone—or several—of the more than 3,044 colleges that accept it.

Volunteer work (as admission factor): Special consideration given to students for activity done on a volunteer basis (e.g., tutoring, hospital care, working with the elderly or disabled) as a service to the community or the public in general.

Waitlist: List of students who meet the admission requirements but will only be offered a place in the class if space becomes available.

Weighted grade point average (GPA): A grade point average calculated using a system that assigns a higher point value to grades in more difficult classes.

Work experience (as admission factor): Special consideration given to students who have been employed prior to application, whether for relevance to major, demonstration of employment-related skills, or as explanation of student's academic and extracurricular record.

FINANCIAL AID DEFINITIONS:

Awarded aid: The dollar amounts offered to financial aid applicants.

External scholarships and grants: Scholarships and grants received from outside (private) sources that students bring with them.

Financial aid applicant: Any applicant who submits any one of the institutionally required financial aid applications/forms, such as the FAFSA.

Financial aid: Money given or loaned to you to help pay for college.

In-state tuition: The tuition charged by institutions to those students who meet the state's or institution's residency requirements.

Institutional scholarships and grants: Endowed scholarships, annual gifts, and tuition-funded grants for which the institution determines the recipient.

Merit grant aid: Scholarships and grants, gifts, or merit-based aid from institutional, state, federal, or other sources (including unrestricted funds or gifts and endowment income) awarded solely on the basis of academic achievement, merit, or any other non-need-based reason.

Need-based aid: College-funded or college-administered awards from institutional, state, federal, or other sources for which a student must have financial need to qualify. This type of financial assistance includes both institutional and noninstitutional student aid (grants, jobs, and loans).

Out-of-state tuition: The tuition charged by institutions to those students who do not meet the institution's or state's residency requirements.

Private student loans: A nonfederal loan made by a lender such as a bank, credit union, or private lender used to pay for up to the annual cost of education, regardless oy any financial aid received.

Work-study and employment: Federal and state work-study aid, as well as any employment packaged by your institution in financial aid awards.

APPENDIX

CHAPTER 1

Bone, Marie-Antonette. "Top 50 Questions to Ask Your School Counselor." *Colleges of Distinction.*
https://collegesofdistinction.com/advice/top-50-questions-to-ask-your-guidance-counselor/

CNBC. "Why experts say the $25 million college admissions scandal is "just the tip of the iceberg." March 13, 2019.
https://www.cnbc.com/2019/03/13/richard-v-reeves-college-admissions-scandal-is-tip-of-the-iceberg.html

College Admissions. "Elements of a strong recommendation letter." August 17, 2014. Video, 2:33.
https://www.youtube.com/watch?v=Zcpwdcvz3KE&t=1s

Cooper, Clay. "Top 35 Questions To Ask Your College Counselor." PrepExpert. December 15, 2017.
https://prepexpert.com/top-35-college-counselor-questions/

Deerfield Academy. "Myths of the Recruiting Process." Accessed May 8, 2020.
https://deerfield.edu/almanac/college-advising/athletic-recruiting-ncaa-eligibility/myths-of-the-recruiting-process/

Goldman, Jordan. "Can HS Guidance counselors reach out directly to college admissions officers?" November 17, 2014. Video, 2:43.
https://www.youtube.com/watch?v=lIBp7kyRlGY

Goldman, Jordan. "Do college admissions officers have relationships with HS guidance counselors?" November 17, 2014. Video, 0:53.
https://www.youtube.com/watch?v=PE2_TIeIBgs

Harvard Faculty of Arts and Sciences. "A message about Harvard Athletics." *Harvard University.* April 4, 2019.
https://www.fas.harvard.edu/news/message-about-harvard-athletics

Her Campus. "The Truth About Counselor Recommendation Letters." *Huffington Post*. October 27, 2014.
https://www.huffpost.com/entry/truth-about-counselor-recommendation-letters_n_6056260

Justice Department. "Affidavit In Support of Criminal Complaint." Accessed June 4, 2020.
https://www.justice.gov/file/1142876/download

Kingsbury, Kathleen. "Dirty Secrets of College Admissions." *Daily Beast*. July 14, 2017.
https://www.thedailybeast.com/dirty-secrets-of-college-admissions

NCAA. "Estimated probability of competing in college athletics." Accessed June 4, 2020.
http://www.ncaa.org/about/resources/research/estimated-probability-competing-college-athletics

Next College Student Athlete. "NCAA Recruiting Rules: When Can College Coaches Contact High School Athletes." Accessed June 4, 2020.
https://www.ncsasports.org/ncaa-eligibility-center/recruiting-rules

Ng, Jonathan. "Admissions consultants warn of red flags." *Boston Herald*. March 12, 2019.
https://www.bostonherald.com/2019/03/12/admissions-consultants-warn-of-red-flags/
https://www.justice.gov/file/1142876/download

Notre Dame Lacrosse. "The Recruiting Series Episode 8: Communication from Recruits to Coaches." April 8, 2020. Video, 2:41.
https://www.youtube.com/watch?v=z7CuUrHw460

Paterson, Jim. "Toward a Better Letter." *NACAC*. Accessed June 4, 2020.
https://www.nacacnet.org/news--publications/journal-of-college-admission/toward-a-better-letter/

Sabky, Rebecca. "Check This Box if You're a Good Person." *The New York Times*. April 4, 2017.
https://www.nytimes.com/2017/04/04/opinion/check-this-box-if-youre-a-good-person.html

Stanford News. "Stanford information on college admissions case." March 14, 2019.
https://news.stanford.edu/2019/03/14/admission-case-info/

Vice News. "How Broken the College Admissions Process Is (HBO)." March 13, 2019. Video, 6:10.
https://www.youtube.com/watch?v=0v5yHnWCiLE

CHAPTER 2

American University Admissions. "What AU Looks For: Demonstrated Interest." September 23, 2019. Video, 2:23.
https://www.youtube.com/watch?v=1VMCAq6PpWw.

Arenson, Karen W. "Thank-You Note Enters College Admission Game." *The New York Times*. October 9, 2007.
https://www.nytimes.com/2007/10/09/education/09thanks.html?campaignId=7JFJX

Boston University. "Alumni Admissions Volunteers—Volunteer Handbook." *Boston University*. 2019-2020.
http://www.bu.edu/admissions/files/2018/06/AAV-Volunteer-Handbook.pdf.

CBS News. "Social media and college admissions." Video, 1:18. *CBS News*.
https://www.youtube.com/watch?v=GyR26v819Nc

College Admissions. "Succeeding at the college admissions interview." August 17, 2014. Video, 6:22.
https://www.youtube.com/watch?v=4qY9icExjEw

https://www.businessinsider.com/college-admissions-advice-interview-2018-11

Jaschik, Scott. "Another Edge for the Wealthy." *Inside Higher Ed*. July 27, 2017.
https://www.insidehighered.com/news/2017/07/27/study-says-common-admissions-practice-measuring-demonstrated-interest-favors.

Kaplan. "College Admissions: The Complete Guide to Social Media."
https://www.kaptest.com/study/college-admissions/college-admission-the-complete-guide-to-social-media/

Koppelman, Caroline. "How to Write a Thank You Note After Your College Tour." *The Koppelman Group*. March 20, 2017.
https://www.koppelmangroup.com/blog/2017/3/20/how-to-write-a-thank-you-note-after-your-college-tour

Moody, Josh. "Why Colleges Look at Students' Social Media." *U.S. News & World Report*. August 22, 2019.
https://www.usnews.com/education/best-colleges/articles/2019-08-22/why-colleges-look-at-students-social-media-accounts

Moon, Kristen. "10 Ways Students Can Use Demonstrated Interest To Their Benefit." *Forbes*. September 17, 2019.
https://www.forbes.com/sites/kristenmoon/2019/09/17/10-ways-students-can-use-demonstrated-interest-to-their-benefit/#71e1c3194431.

Professor Bernstein. "How to Prepare for Yale Alumni Interviews." Video, 7:51.
https://www.youtube.com/watch?v=JYdfUNjyYxo

Shemmassian, Shirag. "6 steps to ace a college interview, according to an expert who worked in Ivy League admissions." *Business Insider*. November 15, 2018.
https://www.businessinsider.in/6-steps-to-ace-a-college-interview-according-to-an-expert-who-worked-in-Ivy-League-admissions/articleshow/66644156.cms

Singer, Natasha. "They Loved Your G.P.A. Then They Saw Your Tweets." *The New York Times*. November 9, 2013.
https://www.nytimes.com/2013/11/10/business/they-loved-your-gpa-then-they-saw-your-tweets.html

Smitobol, Nat. "Tips for College Visit Information Sessions." *Ivywise*. March 24, 2015.
https://blog.ivywise.com/blog-0/tips-for-college-visit-information-sessions.html

Tesh. "Giving Gifts to the Admissions Department Could Actually Hurt Your Chances of Getting into College." *Intelligence for Your Life*. Accessed June 4, 2020. https://www.tesh.com/articles/giving-gifts-to-the-admissions-department-could-actually-hurt-your-chances-of-getting-into-college/

The Princeton Review. "60 Questions To Ask on Your College Tour." https://www.princetonreview.com/college-advice/questions-to-ask-on-a-college-tour

CHAPTER 3

Andersen, Ellen. "What is the Coalition Application?" *College Raptor.* December 20, 2019. https://www.collegeraptor.com/getting-in/articles/questions-answers/what-is-the-coalition-application/

Boyington, Briana, and Josh Moody. "The Common App: Everything You Need to Know." *U.S. News & World Report.* August 1, 2019. https://www.usnews.com/education/best-colleges/articles/common-app

Butterfly, Joel. "7 admissions officers share the things they never tell applicants." *Business Insider.* February 7, 2018. https://www.businessinsider.com/7-things-college-admissions-officers-wish-every-applicant-knew-2018-2

College Coach. "Is it Okay to Apply to College with An Undecided Major?" January 18, 2018. Video, 1:57. https://www.youtube.com/watch?v=EHdZtQbU-H4

Columbia University. "Supplementary Materials." Accessed 2020. https://undergrad.admissions.columbia.edu/apply/first-year/supplementary-materials

Common App. 2020. https://www.commonapp.org/

Dartmouth College. "Supplementary Materials." Accessed 2020. https://admissions.dartmouth.edu/glossary-term/supplemental-materials

Edwards, Halle. "How to Choose a Major for Your College Application." *PrepScholar.* August 25, 2019. https://blog.prepscholar.com/how-to-choose-a-major-for-your-college-application

Franek, Rob. "Should You Submit Supplementary Material to Colleges?" *The Princeton Review.* https://www.princetonreview.com/college-advice/supplementary-material

Goldman, Jordan. "Do college admissions officers pay attention to extra materials students send?" November 17, 2014. Video, 2:14. https://www.youtube.com/watch?v=2vzorTtZjz4

Hartocollis, Anemona. "Harvard's admissions process, once secret, is unveiled in affirmative action trial." *Livemint.* Accessed November 1, 2018. https://www.livemint.com/Politics/dysSlZlq4SD5BxQZH8OqaJ/Harvards-admissions-process-revealed.html

Harvard College. "Admissions Statistics." Accessed 2020.
https://college.harvard.edu/admissions/admissions-statistics

Jaschik, Scott. "Does AP Still Have Admissions Cachet?" *Inside Higher Education.*
June 25, 2018.
https://www.insidehighered.com/admissions/article/2018/06/25/defections-ap-
program-raise-question-whether-it-still-has-admissions

McCammon, Ellen. "AP Scores in College Admissions: Do They Really Matter?"
PrepScholar. March 21, 2020.
https://blog.prepscholar.com/do-colleges-look-at-ap-scores-for-admission

Muniz, Hannah. "Coalition vs Common App: Which Should You Use? *PrepScholar.*
September 8, 2019
https://blog.prepscholar.com/coalition-vs-common-app

Patel, Jason. "5 Easy Ways to Apply to Lots of Colleges at Once." *NICHE.* October 23, 2018.
https://www.niche.com/blog/5-easy-ways-to-apply-to-lots-of-colleges-at-once/

Princeton University. "Optional Arts Supplement." Accessed 2020.
https://admission.princeton.edu/how-apply/application-checklist/optional-arts-form

Rapelye, Janet Lavin. "Part 2: Answers From Princeton's Dean." *The New York Times.*
September 25, 2012.
https://thechoice.blogs.nytimes.com/2012/09/25/guidance-office-princeton-answers-
2/?mtrref=www.google.com&assetType=PAYWALL

The Coalition for College. 2020. *Coalition for College Access.*
http://www.coalitionforcollegeaccess.org/

Veritas Prep College. "Why You Should Take SAT Subject Tests?" March 15, 2016.
Video, 2:47.
https://www.youtube.com/watch?v=ke9j8QYfXxY

Yale University. "Supplementary Materials." Accessed 2020.
https://admissions.yale.edu/supplementary#art

CHAPTER 4

Butterfly, Joel. "7 admissions officers share the things they never tell applicants."
Business Insider. February 7, 2018.
https://www.businessinsider.com/7-things-college-admissions-officers-wish-every-
applicant-knew-2018-2

College Board. "Early Decision & Early Action." Accessed June 4, 2020.
https://professionals.collegeboard.org/guidance/applications/early

College Board. "How Many Applications Are Enough?" Accessed June 4, 2020.
https://professionals.collegeboard.org/guidance/applications/how-many

Kulman, Linda. "How to Get Admissions Officers to Say Yes." *U.S. News & World
Report.* August 21, 2008.

https://www.usnews.com/education/best-colleges/applying/articles/2008/08/21/how-to-get-admissions-officers-to-say-yes

Lifton, Kim. "College Essay Tips from the Admissions Office for your students." *LINK* for Counselors. 2020. https://www.linkforcounselors.com/college-essay-tips-admissions-office-students/

Miller, Karen. "Safety/Level/Reach: 5 Factors in Creating the Best College List for You." *SCOIR*. March 16, 2018. https://www.scoir.com/blog/safety/level/reach-5-factors-in-creating-the-best-college-list-for-you

Pannoni, Alexandra. "What Happens to Students Who Back Out of Early Decision Offers." *U.S. News & World Report.* October 24, 2016. https://www.usnews.com/education/best-colleges/articles/2016-10-24/what-happens-to-students-who-back-out-of-early-decision-offers

Selingo, Jeffrey. "The Two Most Important College-Admissions Criteria Now Mean Less." *The Atlantic.* May 25, 2018. https://www.theatlantic.com/education/archive/2018/05/college-admissions-gpa-sat-act/561167/

Wallace, Jennifer, and Lisa Heffernan. "Advice College Admissions Officers Give Their Own Kids." *The New York Times.* March 17, 2016. https://well.blogs.nytimes.com/2016/03/17/advice-college-admissions-officers-give-their-own-kids/

WowWritingWorkshop. "Tips from the College Admissions Office: Cornell University." October 21, 2013. Video, 2:44. https://www.youtube.com/watch?v=ypH0Ycax8-I

Yale Undergraduate Admissions. "Admissions Advice: Activities." December 5, 2017. Video, 1:53. https://www.youtube.com/watch?v=BFwSLCkxEGM&t=7s

CHAPTER 5

Campus Pride. "Advising LGBTQ Students through the College Admissions Process." May 14, 2013. https://www.campuspride.org/advising-admissions/

College Board. "Advising Undocumented Students." Education Professionals. Accessed April 23, 2020. https://professionals.collegeboard.org/guidance/financial-aid/undocumented-students

Edwards, Halle. "What is a College Legacy? What If You're Not a Legacy?" *PrepScholar.* May 7, 2018. https://blog.prepscholar.com/what-is-a-college-legacy

Helhoski, Anna, and Teddy Nykiel. "Top Scholarships for LGBTQ Students." *NerdWallet.* September 27, 2018. https://www.nerdwallet.com/blog/loans/student-loans/great-lgbt-scholarships/

Korn, Melissa. "How Much Does Being a Legacy Help Your College Admissions Odds?" *The Wall Street Journal*. July 9, 2018. https://www.wsj.com/articles/legacy-preferences-complicate-colleges-diversity-push-1531128601

Liu, Meredith, and Anne Snabes. "A Look Inside How Cornell Accepts Its Students." *The Cornell Daily Sun*. November 6, 2018. https://cornellsun.com/2018/11/06/a-look-inside-how-cornell-accepts-its-students/

Mamlet, Robin, and Christine VanDeVelde. *College Admission: From Application to Acceptance, Step by Step*. (New York: Three Rivers Press, 2011), 344.

Petrow, Steven. "Should a Student Conceal Her Lesbian Identity in College Application Essays?" *The New York Times*. December 3, 2013. https://www.nytimes.com/2013/12/03/booming/should-a-student-conceal-her-lesbian-identity-in-college-application-essays.html

Redford, Jeremy, and Kathleen Mulvaney Hoyer. "First-Generation and Continuing-Generation College Students: A Comparison of High School and Postsecondary Experiences." *US Department of Education*. September 2017. https://nces.ed.gov/pubs2018/2018009.pdf

Reid, Whitelaw. "First-Generation College Student Never Thought He'd Wind Up at UVA." *UVA Today*. January 24, 2018. https://news.virginia.edu/content/first-generation-college-student-never-thought-hed-wind-uva

Rice, Alexandra, and Anna Helhoski. "How DACA Students Can Apply to College." *NerdWallet*. November 9, 2018. https://www.nerdwallet.com/blog/loans/student-loans/undocumented-students-applying-college/

Sharpe, Rochelle. "Are You First Gen? Depends on Who's Asking." *The New York Times*. November 3, 2017. https://www.nytimes.com/2017/11/03/education/edlife/first-generation-college-admissions.html

Stainburn, Samantha. "The Gay Question: Check One." *The New York Times*. July 30, 2013. https://www.nytimes.com/2013/08/04/education/edlife/more-college-applications-ask-about-sexual-identity.html

Stanford University. "Thinking Bigger, Little by Little." *Stanford Magazine*. September/October 2013. https://stanfordmag.org/contents/thinking-bigger-little-by-little

Tate, Allison Slater. "Colleges Welcome Growing Number of Homeschooled Students." *NBC News*. February 17, 2016. https://www.nbcnews.com/feature/college-game-plan/colleges-welcome-growing-number-homeschooled-students-n520126

University of Virginia. "UVA Advice from a First-Generation College Student." December 14, 2017. Video, 0:51. https://www.youtube.com/watch?v=VoY_IbPYR2Q

Worland, Justin C. "LGBT Question May Be Added to Admissions Application." *The Harvard Crimson*. November 16, 2011.
https://www.thecrimson.com/article/2011/11/16/lgbt-admissions-question/

CHAPTER 6

College Confidential. "College experts discuss high school suspensions." June 23, 2010.
https://www.collegeconfidential.com/articles/experts/

CollegeXpress. "30 Questions You Need to Ask Before Choosing a College."
https://www.collegexpress.com/articles-and-advice/admission/articles/find-college/
essential-college-assessment-questions/

Fulbright Belgium, Luxembourg, and EU. "Columbia University: International Admissions." October 13, 2011. Video, 7:44.
https://www.youtube.com/watch?v=gQqGaZ0f2So.

Furda, Eric. "College Admission: Will the Summer Program Help You?" *The University of Pennsylvania.* February 23, 2018.
http://kwhs.wharton.upenn.edu/2018/02/college-admission-will-summer-program-help-you/

Reston, Laura. "College Summer Programs for High Schoolers: Are They Worth It?" *Forbes.* July 1, 2015.
https://www.forbes.com/sites/laurareston/2015/07/01/college-summer-programs-for-high-schoolers-are-they-worth-it/#7831413b4b57

Grove, Allen. "Choosing the Perfect College." *ThoughtCo.* November 30, 2019.
https://www.thoughtco.com/choosing-the-perfect-college-786979

Hillman, Nicholas, and Taylor Weichman. *Education Deserts: The Continued Significance of "Place" in the Twenty-First Century.* Viewpoints: Voices from the Field. Washington, D.C.: *American Council on Education.* 2016. Page 2.

International Baccalaureate. "Do IB Diploma scores influence admissions offers at US colleges and universities?" April 18, 2016. Video, 1:06.
https://www.youtube.com/watch?v=kk6zrCQK6rk

Kowarski, Ilana. "How Your Hometown Could Affect Your College Prospects." *U.S. News & World Report.* September 10, 2018.
https://www.usnews.com/education/best-colleges/articles/2018-09-10/how-your-hometown-could-affect-your-college-admissions-chances

Mamlet, Robin, and Christine VanDeVelde. *College Admission: From Application to Acceptance, Step by Step.* (New York: Three Rivers Press, 2011), 352.

Purtill, Corinne. "If you want to get into an elite college, you might consider moving to one of these states." *QUARTZ.* April 4, 2016.
https://qz.com/653167/if-you-want-to-get-into-an-elite-college-you-might-consider-moving-to-one-of-these-states/

Robin Mamlet and Christine VanDeVelde. College Admission: From Application to Acceptance, Step by Step. (New York: Three Rivers Press, 2011).

Unigo. "Does your hometown have any effect on your chances of getting in?"
Accessed April 23, 2020.
https://www.unigo.com/admissions-advice/does-your-hometown-have-any-effect-on-your-chances-of-getting-in/65/1

US-UK Fulbright Commission. "Application Tips from Yale University." September
19, 2010. Video, 10:17.
https://www.youtube.com/watch?v=5kaAsZyMC4Y

UT Admissions Guy. "UT-Austin Admissions Tip #14: International Applicants."
July 25, 2016. Video, 8:18.
https://www.youtube.com/watch?v=GdYyvcVA3l4

CHAPTER 7

CollegeXpress. "30 Questions You Need to Ask Before Choosing a College."
Accessed May 3, 2020.
https://www.collegexpress.com/articles-and-advice/admission/articles/find-college/essential-college-assessment-questions/

Farrell, Elizabeth F. "Behind the Scenes, Admissions Offices Conquer Mounds of
Mail." *The Chronicle of Higher Education*. January 25, 2008.
https://www-chronicle-com.proxy.library.georgetown.edu/article/Behind-the-Scenes-Admissions/26648

Grove, Allen. "Choosing the Perfect College." *ThoughtCo*. November 30, 2019.
https://www.thoughtco.com/choosing-the-perfect-college-786979

Harberson, Sara. "Op-Ed: The truth about "holistic" college admissions." *Los
Angeles Times*. June 9, 2015.
https://www.latimes.com/opinion/op-ed/la-oe-harberson-asian-american-admission-rates-20150609-story.html

Heimbach, Alex. "What Do Ivy League Schools Think of the ACT? *PrepScholar*.
March 15, 2018.
https://blog.prepscholar.com/what-do-ivy-league-schools-think-of-the-act

NCAA Eligibility Center. "2018-2019 Guide for Four-Year Transfers: For Student
athletes at Four-Year Colleges." Accessed June 4, 2020.
http://www.ncaapublications.com/productdownloads/TGONLINE42018.pdf

Peterson, Chris. "Missing Documents Due Monday." *MIT Admissions*. January 26, 2012.
https://mitadmissions.org/blogs/entry/missing-documents-due-monday/

Pippen, Carolyn. "Lessons from a Departing Admissions Counselor." *Vanderbilt
University*. May 29, 2014.
https://admissions.vanderbilt.edu/vandybloggers/2014/05/lessons-from-a-departing-admissions-counselor/

Shannon-Karasik, Caroline. "Did You Miss a College Application Deadline?"
Campus Explorer. Accessed May 3, 2020.
https://www.campusexplorer.com/college-advice-tips/5D72B251/Did-You-Miss-a-College-Application-Deadline/

Shoreline. "How to transfer from a community college to a four-year? Recruiters give advice." October 16, 2014. Video, 2:31.
https://www.youtube.com/watch?v=VU78shwgc9A

UMass Amherst Admissions. "What is holistic review? Freshman Admissions 101." July 12, 2019. Video, 2:13.
https://www.youtube.com/watch?v=nQNTJH_vI8c

Wallace, Jennifer, and Lisa Heffernan. "Advice College Admissions Officers Give Their Own Kids." *The New York Times.* March 17, 2016.
https://well.blogs.nytimes.com/2016/03/17/advice-college-admissions-officers-give-their-own-kids/

Yale Undergraduate Admissions. "Holistic Review." October 28, 2015. Video, 2:23.
https://www.youtube.com/watch?v=cTNe4olFxuw

CHAPTER 8

Adler, Kevin F. "My Successful Letter of Appeal to UC Berkeley." *Huffington Post.* May 25, 2013.
https://www.huffingtonpost.com/kevin-f-adler/college-decision-appeals_b_2918586.html

Allan, Laura. "When Not to Appeal Your Admission Decision." Accessed May 8, 2020.
https://study.com/articles/When_To_Appeal_Your_Admission_Decision.html

College Admissions. "Selecting Your College." August 17, 2014. Video, 1:21.
https://youtu.be/q71hYD9Xhek

College Board. "Application Ethics." Accessed May 8, 2020.
https://professionals.collegeboard.org/guidance/applications/ethics

College Board. "Senioritis." Accessed June 5, 2020.
https://professionals.collegeboard.org/guidance/applications/senioritis

College Board. "Wait-Listed & Rejected Students." Accessed May 8, 2020.
https://professionals.collegeboard.org/guidance/applications/rejected

DeNuccio, Kyle. "A College Application Guide for Gap Year Students." *The New York Times.* April 6, 2017.
https://www.nytimes.com/2017/04/06/education/edlife/a-college-application-guide-for-gap-year-students.html

Finder, Alan. "Admissions Officials Lament Practice of Signing On With More than One College." *The New York Times.* May 20, 2006.
https://www.nytimes.com/2006/05/20/us/20deposit.html

Goldman, Jordan. "Do colleges ever revoke offers of admissions? If so, why?" November 17, 2014. Video, 4:07.
https://www.youtube.com/watch?v=Rv5C8_kLSxI

Goldman, Jordan. "How can college applicants get accepted off the waitlist?" November 17, 2014. Video, 1:24.
https://www.youtube.com/watch?v=pantYqSP8jE

Grove, Allen. "Can You Appeal a College Rejection?" ThoughtCo. May 1, 2020.
https://www.thoughtco.com/can-you-appeal-a-college-rejection-788870

Haverford College. "Who should apply Early Decision?" October 1, 2018. Video, 1:23.
https://www.youtube.com/watch?v=HPLxLoy-Ens

Jerome-Alexander, Evelyn. "Some Ethical Issues in College Admissions." Magellan
College Counseling. February 21, 2019.
https://magellancounseling.com/ethical-issues/

McGann, Matt. "On taking a 'Gap Year.'" MIT Admissions. April 11, 2011.
https://mitadmissions.org/blogs/entry/on_taking_a_gap_year_2/

Middlebury College. "Taking a Gap Year."
http://www.middlebury.edu/admissions/apply/decisions/gapyearinfo

Moody, Josh. "A Guide to the College Admissions Appeal Process." *U.S. News &
World Report.* March 6, 2020.
https://www.usnews.com/education/best-colleges/articles/a-guide-to-the-college-
admissions-appeal-process

Roll, Nick. "The Malia Impact: Counselors Consider Growing Interest in Gap Years."
Inside Higher Ed. September 25, 2017.
https://www.insidehighered.com/admissions/article/2017/09/25/admissions-
counselors-consider-growing-interest-gap-years

Timsit, Annabelle. "The case against the college waitlist." *QUARTZ.* March 31, 2019.
https://qz.com/1582265/what-getting-waitlisted-for-college-actually-means-now/

Webster, Emma Sarran. "How to Write an Appeal Letter for College Admissions
Rejections: 8 Ways to Make Your Case." *Teen Vogue.* February 4, 2019.
https://www.teenvogue.com/story/how-to-appeal-college-rejection

CHAPTER 9

Andersen, Ellen. "How to Avoid College Application Fees." College Raptor. January
23, 2020.
https://www.collegeraptor.com/getting-in/articles/college-applications/how-to-
avoid-college-application-fees/

Clark, Kim. "Colleges Where Need for Aid Can Hurt Admission Odds. *U.S. News &
World Report.* March 23, 2010.
https://www.usnews.com/education/articles/2010/03/23/colleges-where-need-for-
aid-can-hurt-admission-odds

College Admissions. "Cost of in-state vs out-of-state tuition." February 8, 2016. Video, 1:36.
https://www.youtube.com/watch?v=wRPJKDtoZNs

College Board. "Application fee waiver." NACAC. Accessed June 5, 2020. www.
nacacnet.org/studentinfo/feewaiver/Pages/default.aspx

College Board. "College Application Fee Waiver FAQs." Accessed May 8, 2020.
https://bigfuture.collegeboard.org/get-in/applying-101/college-application-fee-waivers

College Essay Guy. "How to Write a Great Financial Aid Appeal Letter."
https://www.collegeessayguy.com/blog/financial-aid-appeal-letter

Colorado State University. "Do I Qualify for a Fee Waiver or Enrollment Deposit Deferral?" Accessed May 8, 2020.
https://admissions.colostate.edu/2017/02/27/qualify-fee-waiver-enrollment-deposit-deferral/

Ezarik, Melissa. "Busted: Six top myths of in-state tuition eligibility." Bankrate. August 15, 2005.
https://www.bankrate.com/finance/money-guides/busted-six-top-myths-of-in-state-tuition-eligibility-1.aspx

Finder, Alan. "Admissions Officials Lament Practice of Signing On With More Than One College." *The New York Times*. May 20, 2006.
https://www.nytimes.com/2006/05/20/us/20deposit.html

Get Me to College. "Fee Waivers for Transfer Students' College Applications." Accessed June 5, 2020.
https://getmetocollege.org/fee-waivers-for-transfer-students-college-applications

Gillies, Trent. "Filling in the gap year after high school: Making the most of time off." *CNBC*. May 15, 2016.
https://www.cnbc.com/2016/05/14/filling-in-the-gap-year-after-high-school-making-the-most-of-time-off.html

Grown and Flown. "Here is the Real Cost of Applying to College." January 31, 2018.
https://grownandflown.com/real-cost-applying-college/

Horovitz, Bruce. "Colleges hidden costs: What the admissions office doesn't tell you." *The Washington Post*. November 26, 2016.
https://www.washingtonpost.com/business/colleges-hidden-costs-what-the-admissions-office-doesnt-tell-you/2016/11/25/5531a0e8-b02a-11e6-be1c-8cec35b1ad25_story.html

Kantrowitz, Mark. "How to Appeal for More Financial Aid for College." *Saving for College*. January 21, 2019.
https://www.savingforcollege.com/article/how-to-appeal-for-more-financial-aid-for-college

Kerr, Emma. "How to Write a Financial Aid Appeal Letter." *U.S. News & World Report*. April 10, 2019.
https://www.usnews.com/education/best-colleges/paying-for-college/articles/2019-04-10/how-to-write-a-financial-aid-appeal-letter

LoveToKnow. "Financial Aid Appeal Letter."
https://cf.ltkcdn.net/college/files/2763-financial-aid-appeal-letter.pdf

Powell, Farran. "3 Facts About Aid, Tuition for Out-of-State Students." *U.S. News & World Report*. October 24, 2016.
https://www.usnews.com/education/best-colleges/paying-for-college/articles/2016-10-24/3-facts-about-aid-tuition-for-out-of-state-students

Scott, Amy. "Forget tuition, just applying to college can cost thousands."
Marketplace. April 1, 2013.
https://www.marketplace.org/2013/04/01/forget-tuition-just-applying-college-can-cost-thousands/

The Stanford Daily. "Plan for need-blind admissions for international students."
March 9, 2018.
https://www.stanforddaily.com/2018/03/09/op-ed-plan-for-need-blind-admissions-for-international-students/

WXYZ-TV Detroit. "In-state tuition for out-of-state students." October 3, 2017. Video, 2:12.
https://www.youtube.com/watch?v=VU9Gb7jpp_c

CHAPTER 10

Alzahrani, Mohsen. "U.S. Financial Aid Options for International Students." World
Education Services. January 16, 2019.
https://www.wes.org/advisor-blog/u-s-financial-aid-for-international-students/

College Board. "The College Board's Net Price Calculator." Accessed May 8, 2020.
https://professionals.collegeboard.org/higher-ed/financial-aid/netprice

Cranshaw, Cordelia. "Student Voice: The long road out of foster care included beauty
pageants — and lots of studying." *The Hechinger Report.* July 1, 2019.
https://hechingerreport.org/student-voice-high-school-and-foster-care/

Davidson College. "Using the Net Price Calculator." October 4, 2011. Video, 2:29.
https://www.youtube.com/watch?v=2NZUag1EuZY

Federal Student Aid. "Complete the FAFSA Form."
https://studentaid.ed.gov/sa/fafsa

GPA Interactive. "Can an International Student get a Job While in the U.S.?"
December 9, 2014. Video, 2:37.
https://www.youtube.com/watch?v=VxeNZxrIH3M

GPA Interactive. "Financial Aid Opportunities for International Students." March
3, 2015. Video, 0:50.
https://www.youtube.com/watch?v=EGFzZo4JDOY

Harvard College. "Net Price Calculator." Griffin Financial Aid Office.
https://college.harvard.edu/financial-aid/net-price-calculator

Kerr, Emma. "What to Know About a College's Net Price Calculator." *U.S. News &
World Report.* May 8, 2019.
https://www.usnews.com/education/best-colleges/paying-for-college/articles/2019-05-08/what-to-know-about-a-colleges-net-price-calculator

Lockwood, Andy. "3 Deadly FAFSA Mistakes." February 9, 2011. Video, 4:43.
https://www.youtube.com/watch?v=edtGrqeiDeM

Nykiel, Teddy. "Applying for Financial Aid for College: 6 Tips from Counselors." *Nerd Wallet.* March 18, 2019.
https://www.nerdwallet.com/blog/loans/student-loans/college-counselors-financial-aid/

Rashed, Kesha. "From Foster Care to College." Affordable College Online. Accessed May 8, 2020.
https://www.affordablecollegesonline.org/college-resource-center/foster-care-to-college/

Rosen, Steve. "Not enough parents realize the importance of FAFSA. Here's what families of college kids should know." *Chicago Tribune.* August 22, 2019.
https://www.chicagotribune.com/lifestyles/parenting/ct-life-fafsa-what-to-know-0822-20190822-l7afomuaubhhpcck52r7shrhmu-story.html

Smith-Barrow, Delece. "From foster care to college." *The Hechinger Report.* December 1, 2018.
https://hechingerreport.org/from-foster-care-to-college/

Soriano, Deborah Ziff. "3 Myths About Army ROTC Scholarships for College." *U.S. News & World Report.* March 4, 2020.
https://www.usnews.com/education/best-colleges/paying-for-college/articles/2017-06-14/3-myths-about-army-rotc-scholarships-for-college

The FAFSA Guru. "3 FAFSA secrets to help you get the most financial aid." September 26, 2017. Video, 5:40.
https://www.youtube.com/watch?v=iiPozmLjQiw

The University of Massachusetts Amherst. "Army ROTC."
https://www.umass.edu/armyrotc/about/frequently-asked-questions-faq

US Army. Army ROTC. Accessed June 5, 2020.
https://www.goarmy.com/rotc/high-school-students/four-year-scholarship.html

US Department of Education. "Foster Care Transition Toolkit." Washington, D.C. May 26, 2016.
https://www2.ed.gov/about/inits/ed/foster-care/youth-transition-toolkit.pdf

Unigo. "What Financial Aid Is Available for International Students?" *U.S. News & World Report.* January 4, 2012.
https://www.usnews.com/education/blogs/college-admissions-experts/2012/01/04/what-financial-aid-is-available-for-international-students

Yale Undergraduate Admissions. "Yale's Net Price Calculator." October 27, 2015. Video, 2:39.
https://www.youtube.com/watch?v=MrKmK32bWcs

GLOSSARY

Common Data Set Initiative. CDS Publishers. Accessed June 5, 2020.
https://www.commondataset.org/

College Board. "College Admission Glossary: Learn the Lingo." Accessed June 5, 2020.

Made in the USA
Las Vegas, NV
05 May 2021

22551204R00134